MW01124420

P◖WER
Moms

Diane
you are more powerful
than you know!

POWER Moms

Persevere

Overcome

Win

Empower

Restore

Author: Sherrie Walton

Co-Authors: Dr. LaTonya Woodson, Jaquithia Stinson, Shantania Leggins, Mary Smith, Dr. Kanini Brooks, Trina Smith, Shirley Walker-King, Shakeena Brantley, Katrina Hudson, Anita Bowman Roussel, Tashara Robinson

Sherrie Walton Publishing Group, LLC

www.iamsherriewalton.com

admin@iamsherriewalton.com

Ordering Information:

Go to www.powermomsbook.com or

email thepowermoms@gmail.com

Printed in the United States of America

ISBN-13: 978-1-63227-214-0

We would like to dedicate this book to Moms all over the world.

You are Appreciated, you are Loved… you are Amazing.

The POWER Moms

#IamaPowerMom

Table of Contents:

Introduction:

Introduction:

The POWER Moms book is written to help you discover your true identity, purpose and power. The stories you'll read here cover the highest highs and lowest lows of women just like you, that tapped into their God given Power to create the life they could only dream of. You'll connect with them as they tell you the raw truth of how they triumphed over seemingly insurmountable odds and achieved unprecedented levels of success, peace and freedom.

The women writers in this book are successful business advisers, entrepreneurs, consultants, public speakers and life coaches. These women are not just inspirations in the business world and in their community, but they are inspirations in the home as well. They have managed to find that perfect balance between a booming career and a strong, loving motherhood, the secrets to which they're more than happy to share inside.

POWER Moms differs from similar books you may have come across for one good reason- other books know the what, but POWER Moms knows the why. POWER Moms is different because it knows why you, the reader, are looking at self-help books.

Maybe you've had a rough few months at work.

Maybe you've been through a rough patch in your home life.

Maybe you just feel like you're in a rut and want to climb out and back into the world at large.

Whatever the case may be, POWER Moms understands.

The women profiled within have been there, in these exact situations and made it out the other side for the better. This book makes no claims or promises, save for one:

POWER Moms is here to help.

Where do you find your POWER?

I find my POWER from within. God has truly given me a "I can't quit" tenacity and I tap into this when things get hard. I also find my POWER in my purpose. I have an aggressive vision to touch the lives of over 1 million women. I will keep going until I reach that. Every day I wake up with this goal in mind. God gives me the power to keep going and living life to the best of my ability.

Chapter 1

The POWER Within

> "**If there is no enemy within**, the **enemy** outside can do you **no** harm.
>
> "~ African Proverb"

I've never met a woman that didn't wear multiple capes (roles) in her life, her significant other's life, her kids' lives, her friends' lives, her clients' lives...and the list goes on and on. We (I include myself also) wear these capes for everyone, knowing that it's humanly impossible for us to save the world. We know that we don't possess the capabilities or the "superpowers" to save everyone and everything. Yet, we try. Our attempts often leave us feeling overwhelmed, frustrated and unappreciated. But, it's our own fault. We overextend ourselves and misinterpret our strength. We believe that we're strong for the sake of carrying everyone and their problems on our shoulders. We try to fix it for everyone, and in the end, we're left feeling broken, battered, bruised and betrayed. The truth is, our strength is given as a gift to us, to help carry out the purpose for our own lives. Our strength is given to us to help overcome the obstacles we face. Our strength is given to us to help overcome the fear and self-doubt that appears from time to time to delay us from our purpose.

⏻ My Ugly Reality

One day I had to come face to face with my reality. It was UGLY. I didn't want to deal with it. Having to put my big girl panties on forced me to take responsibility for my life. I had been in denial for years. Maybe it was the superwoman cape all battered and torn that I (begrudgingly) put on every morning as I rolled out of bed. Maybe it was the fact that I had failed at my business a few times, and the thought of trying again frightened me. Or maybe it was the fact that I had finally become tired and worn out with life itself. I was discouraged, depressed and broken. Life had smacked me with a hard blow and years later I found myself in a cycle of "stuck" trying to piece my life together and rebuild my word. It was a difficult season. Many days I would sit and daydream about a better life. But this time, I didn't know if I had the strength to bounce back. I was existing in "stucks-ville" sorting between the reality of my life and the dreams I had tucked away thinking maybe I had missed my season. I was stuck watching everything I knew that I deserved escape from me. Something wasn't working, the dots weren't connecting and as I put on this invisible cape every day for my husband, my kids and my friends…I silently cried. Everyone always assumed that I was the strong one. I had been strong for so long no one felt the need to rescue me. The truth is I didn't want to be strong. But, I felt like I didn't have a choice. It was either be strong or die. I must admit I appeared tough on the exterior but in reality, I was a woman that wanted to be loved, held, appreciated, understood, and catered to. I just didn't know how to ask for help. As women we all want someone to protect us and love us. We want to feel safe and secure--we don't want to be our own superhero.

 ## Leap of Faith

The year my business failed was one of the hardest things I'd ever had to face. I was on top of the world one minute and the next I was losing everything. The embarrassment, the humiliation, and the constant "you messed up" reminders from those closest to me made me feel like a total failure. Before I became a Full-time Entrepreneur, I'd worked in Corporate America. I was the youngest African American Insurance Broker at a Fortune 500 Company in Miami. I was on top of it all. I climbed the corporate ladder going from a temporary employee to securing a corner office and a 200% pay raise in 3 years. I was unstoppable. But even after achieving this I was still not fully enjoying life. There was a constant tug inside of me to do more. I had a steady pull in my heart to become an Entrepreneur. I was already in business part-time, but I wanted to be in total control of my schedule. I wanted to be available for my husband and kids. I wanted to be there for my clients when they needed me. I wanted to be the Boss. It's amazing how we have these indicators in our spirit that pull us towards our purpose. I suppressed the push in my spirit as long as I could and finally decided that it was time for me to take that leap. With no formal plan in place (big mistake) I decided to enter the world of full-time Entrepreneurship.

I had no fear about it. I knew that my business would be successful. I had always been an overachiever, extremely competitive and a quick-skilled learner. My parents instilled in me the attitude that I could do anything I put my mind to. I knew how to create ways to make money. However, what I lacked were the necessary skills needed to manage my finances and foresee business trends and forecasts. These are essential components to operating a successful business. Had I taken the time to learn or sit under a mentor, I probably wouldn't have made such significant financial mistakes. Everything came at me so fast, the money, the notoriety, and the celebrity clientele. I had finally arrived. While I was living my life, I stopped checking in with God every day. I was too busy, and surely he understood I was making a better life for my family and me. *Or maybe He didn't.*

At the time everything hit the fan, I had been in full-time business a few years. I had an office, staff, and partnerships with some of the most prominent hotel chains and retailers, earning features in a few publications. When the rug was snatched from underneath me, I wasn't prepared mentally or spiritually to deal with it. *Sure, everyone goes through hard times*, I thought to myself. *I will bounce back from this and be on top, like always.* Almost two years passed, and I wasn't able to get my stride. I wasn't able to dig myself out of the financial hole, and everything we had built came crashing down. We lost everything that we were accustomed to, the

12

house, the Mercedes, and the lifestyle. My world as I knew it was over. Unable to save myself, and too prideful to ask for help, I fell into a deep depression. Every day was a struggle for me to stay alive. I existed for my husband and kids, but secretly I wished I could end the pain.

My inner superhero had lost her strength. I was weak. I needed a hero. After a few years and a move to a new state, God began dealing with me about finding my POWER. I didn't even know where to start. I had no desire to ever be in business again. I had lost my passion for success. I didn't want to be great. I just wanted to hide away. I asked God to leave me alone and find someone else that was worthy of the purpose He had shown me over and over again in my dreams. Self-sabotage became a coping mechanism. It was a cover-up for the depression that I was secretly experiencing. I self-sabotaged in every way that I could. Self- sabotage was my way of delaying my purpose. It was an inner ticking time bomb that surfaced just as my next level of greatness was knocking on my door.

Self-sabotage and I had become great friends…sort of. We had a tumultuous relationship. We loved each other hard and hated each other even harder. It was there for me at my lowest times, allowing me to wallow in my self-pity.

It showed up in many different ways in my life. Things for my family started turning, around but every time I was on the brink of a new big deal, I would self-sabotage. I started doing things like *Overthinking… Procrastinating… Moving at a snail's pace… Not giving my best… Rehearsing all of my screw ups… Not completing anything… Not nurturing great relationships… Not showing up at all… Not following through… you know, the usual stuff.* I was determined to be "normal."

She is clothed with strength and dignity, and she laughs without fear of the future. Proverbs 16:25

The day I tripped over my Fearlessness was during one of the hardest times of my life. At the time I was writing my first book and my family, and I were living in a motel. It had gotten really bad for us financially. It was so bad that a few times when we ran out of money for the motel we would sleep in the car. We were homeless. I had never been so low in my life. Help was just a phone call away, but God wouldn't let me reach out to my family or my husband's family to help us. He loudly spoke to me and told me that this was my 'life' lesson. There were things He needed me to learn about myself before it was time for my purpose to be birthed. He wanted me to know what it meant to rely on Him as my source - not my resume, not my connections and not my bank account. I had to learn to grow my faith and depend and rely on Him. It was tough. I cried a lot. I was a spoiled girl in a woman's body used to having the finer things and life, and now here I was forced to purchase food, pampers, and anything else we needed from the Dollar store.

I had to stand up and take responsibility for my role in my life. I had to take responsibility for the bad financial decisions I'd made. At the time I blamed everyone. It was everyone's fault- my husband, my kids, my friends, my family. I refused to take responsibility for my life and my actions until the day I looked in the mirror, and the mirror talked back to me. Yes, it sounds a bit strange to hear myself repeat it- but that's what happened to me. The woman in the mirror asked me, *What are you going to do with yourself? When are you going to get up and present to the world what they need? When are you going to stop hiding in shame and running from your purpose?*

I realized at that moment; I had previously stopped looking at myself in the mirror. I had stopped talking to myself in the mirror because I knew what that meant. I knew I would have to dig past all the layers of disappointment and find the real me. The strong Me, the one that believed in my dream before 'life' told me I couldn't do it. The strong Me, that one that carried me when others told me I couldn't do it. She was in there. I used to celebrate when we won. She and I hadn't talked to each other in so long; we had practically become strangers. That day I decided to be the Fearless woman that God had called me to me. That day I decided to re-discover my POWER.

My life purpose has allowed me to share the stage with some amazing women with impressive resumes. I have learned that we all share a common bond to fight and win at life no matter what is thrown our way. I believe there is greatness inside of everyone. But we must know that greatness doesn't exempt us from taking life's tests. No matter who you are or where you from, life is always going to require something from you before you reach your next level.

If you have found yourself wondering why life is always turning you upside down or wondering why it's so hard for you to catch a break, you're in the right place. Like me, you have to accept a few things.

► Life is always teaching us a lesson about ourselves. The lessons show us who we are, and not just who we think we are. The lessons show us our character; they show us our strengths and our weaknesses. Being taught a lesson by life isn't a bad thing…it's a necessary thing.

► You can't rush your process; you must endure it. Oh, how we wish we could take the crash course or read the cliff notes on life as we did in college. Our microwave, fast food lifestyles motivate us to want everything fast and exactly the way we want it. You can't buy your way out of the process, talk your way out of it or take the shortcut. You must walk through it step by step.

► "Every dog has its Day." Now, please don't get offended. I am not calling you a dog. I am simply saying that everyone has a process, a story and a season. No one is exempt from the seasons of life. Life has taught me to be less judgmental of others. Since everyone has their process and season, I have learned to be careful how I speak to, and about people. Today it could be them going through a difficulty; tomorrow it could be me.

I'm sure everyone can relate to the fear that surmounts when you start a new project, start a new venture, or decide you want to better your life. Fear's entire purpose is to keep you from tapping into your full potential. You are not the only one that deals with this. We all have a familiar comfortable (and sometimes uncomfortable) place that speaks to us and tries to convince us to stay stuck. Everyone has to overcome self-sabotage. Everyone has to look at in the mirror and deal with it head-on.

Discovering Purpose

Can I ask you a question? Have you discovered your purpose? Are you interested in showing up big in your life? As a life coach, I encounter so many amazing women that are living their lives less than their potential. I attribute some of that to fear. The other side of that I attribute to women trying to be Superheroes for everyone else but forgetting to put on their own oxygen mask. Can I bring this home to you? Could it be the reason you stay busy with so many idle things is that you have no idea what you're supposed to be doing with your life? Sure, you're a great Mom…but what else? Sure, you're a great employee…but what's next? How big do you show up in your own life? How often do you step away from everything and everyone to spend time with God to make sure you're on track? Let's back up a little bit; I don't want to get ahead of myself. My question to you is… *Have you discovered your purpose? Have you discovered what you have been created to do? Have you discovered that thing God talks about that He put on the inside of you before you were born?*

I can assure you that once you discover that "thing," you'll live your life differently. You'll make better decisions for your life. You'll start to seem a little more selfish with your time and energy... you'll learn how to say "no" to anything that doesn't align with it. When I re-discovered my purpose, I became a woman on a mission. I wrote my book, I launched my Mommy & Me Tour, I started a Mom's support organization, and I started coaching women to find their greatness. When God showed me my purpose, I pursued it full force.

So, I can hear you through the pages. *How do I find my purpose?* If you have ever watched a mystery or suspense movie, you'll notice a few things in each one. You'll see that before you can solve the mystery, you have to look at the clues. Throughout each scene of the movie, there is a little something in the plot that's revealed. You must pay close attention to the clues because if you don't, you'll miss something...you'll miss an important detail needed to solve the story. *What clues has life revealed to you about yourself that you've been missing?*

Finding your purpose will be simpler than you think once you re-discover who you are. Let's be upfront and confront a few things. We are all guilty at some point and time of making choices in our life reflective of the current situation we are in. Let me explain myself a little more. If you are in a married or dating relationship and your significant other says they want you to wear a certain type of clothes, whether you are totally in love with the outfit or not, you will put it on to make them happy. Why do we do this? I believe we have an inner mechanism that wants to please others. We like it when people are happy with us. Some of us change so much for people that that one day we look in the mirror and ask ourselves… "Who are you?" To tap into your purpose and your POWER, you must know who you are. Not what you majored in… not what society has influenced you to be… not who your friends want you to be… and not who your family wants you to be… Who are you?

 ## The Discovery

Let me ask you this, *What do you do well?* A better way to ask this is, What do you do effortlessly? Take some time to mediate and think about this. What are people always asking you to do for them? What have you been doing since a child that has come naturally to you? Everyone isn't gifted to sing, or act or play a professional sport… some people are gifted at serving, others at talking, and some at administration. No one gift (or person) is better than the next. So again I ask you, What are you gifted at doing? And are you sitting on those gifts in fear of them not being "good enough" to compare to others? Are you ready to go on the road to discovery… the road to your true freedom?

 ## Layers of Purpose.

When I think of layers of purpose, I think about this amazing Nacho dip my husband Chris makes. He includes over seven different layers of gooey yumminess layered with ground beef, tomatoes, guacamole, olives, sour cream, refried beans, topped with melted cheese and sour cream. It's so delicious. Each time you dip into it you discover another mouthful of deliciousness. No two bites are the same... that's how it is with our lives. We're layered together by so many of our experiences that we create yummy gooeyness when dipped into.

Your purpose will be revealed in little nuggets over time. It's pretty amazing when you think about it, but it's like digging for treasure. Discovering your purpose is not an overnight process. Up until this point in your life, your past has shaped what you see when you look in the mirror. Your friends, your family, and people that you have considered authority figures in life, have given you their opinions about what they feel you should or should not be doing. Most time out of their fears, they shape us and aid us in creating self-limiting beliefs about ourselves; scaring us into shying away from the things that thrust us out of our comfort zone. Your purpose is a culmination of your experiences both good and bad. It will take you spending some time alone with God to discover all of the pieces. Finding it will be like solving a riddle of a puzzle. Once you find it, you will know.

⏻   Life Leaves Clues

When I was 17, I was elected Senior Class President... Now today I lead and coach women all around the world. When I was 18, I gave my first speech at my high school graduation in front of 2,000+ attendees... at 40 I was offered a speaking opportunity that opened the door for me to host my first tour. At 28, I launched my first event planning company... today I plan events for myself and others. At 33, I became a Mother... now I'm able to connect with Moms and help them tell their stories. Do you see how it all started to connect? At 31, I worked as an Insurance Broker... now I negotiate major contracts for my business. At 21, I was asked to edit an Employee's Manual for a corporation... Now I help others write their books. It was never in my plans to be a Mother, a Speaker, a Leader, a Writer or a Conference Host. God knew differently. My life had been leaving me clues and when I finally slowed down to connect the dots and get over my "woe is me" mentality, I was able to discover my purpose. I now travel and train other women how to discover their purpose and POWER within. What clues has life been leaving you?

One of my greatest desires is that you would discover your power within you. It breaks my heart to see so many women existing in life and not fulfilling their destiny. If you are not careful you will lose yourself. If you are not careful you will miss your appointment with destiny. I pray as you continue to read through the pages of this book that you will find your will and the POWER within to win. God has given each of us a gift, it's up to us to unwrap it and use it. Tap into your P. O. W. E. R.

Persevere : To persist in a state, enterprise, or undertaking in spite of counter influences, opposition, or discouragement.*

Overcome : To get the better of or to gain the superiority.*

Win : To be successful or victorious. *

Empower : To make (someone) stronger and more confident, especially in controlling their life and claiming their rights*

Restore : To return (someone or something) to a former condition, place, or position*

* Definitions found in Merriam Webster Dictionary

Always remember, the biggest battle you will ever fight will be within. The biggest fear you will ever encounter is your own. The most critical person you will ever meet is yourself. You have the POWER within you to shape your life and live out your purpose. You have the POWER to save yourself. I can attest that when you are ready for your next level in life, God will send you the right people to direct you there. Now go be Fearless!

Meet Dr. LaTonya Woodson

Where do you find your POWER?

I find my POWER with a constant combination of faith and forgiveness, staying focused, family, fortitude and fun! If any of these important elements are missing in my life at any time, there is an obvious void and the emotional toll is great. This impact is personal and beyond, as it manifests itself in my relationships with God, my family and friends and my work. Because of my tenacious spirit, even when I've been knocked down (figuratively), I don't stay down. God gives me the strength, the courage and the POWER to get up and keep fighting to victory!!

Chapter 2

The Face of Perseverance

"And not only that, but we also glory in tribulations, knowing that tribulation produces perseverance; and perseverance, character; and character, hope." Romans 5:3-4

When women look at me, they see the perfect life. The happy marriage, the successful corporate career, the Ph.D., "and" the School Board election win. However, if there's an audition for someone to be the poster child for a "perseverance" ad, I'll gladly and proudly raise my hand high. Make that both hands, so that I can clap loudly and give God praise. If you're like me and, most likely, more than half of the human race, you've had to press your way through a tough situation a time or two. By press, I mean when you really have had to be patient and vigilant at the same time. You've had to smile in the face of others and just moments later cry like a baby behind closed doors. Maybe you've had to play Chess with your bank accounts to cover overspent or unforgotten credit card charges or written checks only to find your time has expired. Or you may have had to make a call to your boss asking him or her to add some extra hours to your schedule to pay for your child's piano lesson, school uniform or dance recital costume. In either case, your mind escalates to full throttle mode without resting for one minute because you are determined to be a survivor, an overcomer. In other words, you simply don't give up. It's how you're naturally wired or, perhaps, through the years you've learned to adapt to constant change. It's a stretch, but you work tirelessly to get through your situation. Some of those situations are minor, like having to stretch a few dollars for a whole week or running out of gas or getting a flat tire on your way to work. Perhaps, even those examples have elevated to the major leagues. They may not be so minor after all. When you've got five or six mouths to feed at home, and an unpaid utility bill during that stretch, equating a situation like any of those as minor is a huge understatement. In dire situations, like losing a job because you were late to work because of that flat tire -- on a day that just happened to be the last straw for your unsympathetic boss -- you must immediately amp your energy level and devise a new plan of action. It doesn't matter that just on yesterday or last week, you had to persevere through a different kind of stressful situation. For many of us, including me, when you get over a hump or a catastrophic event or, simply put, when you solve that one problem, you have a gut feeling that some new circumstance or malaise is lurking just around the corner. You have no idea how tough or how long this next round of misery will be. You only know that you've got to gear up, go to battle and come out victorious.

As a Mother, I can tell you what it was like to wake up several hours during the night and instantly discern which type of baby's cry I had to respond to. Was it the cry of hunger or the cry of sickness or one of the many other cries we've learned to decipher? Only a Mother can tell you what it's like to get a call from the school and have your heart drop before learning that your child is either sick or in trouble. It's usually one of the two. Those are the tests of Mothers, and they can share their testimonies to other Mothers or other Mothers-to-be because of their real-life experiences. Although with good intentions, I'm sure, women without children cannot fully understand what it's like raising children compared to women who have experienced the joys and sorrows of raising children.

Again, we press our way through tests like all those tests that have come before, adding a little more strength, a little more endurance, a little more power to keep going. Our circumstances, trials or tests make us stronger each time we go through them. The beauty of this is knowing that we will come through them and not get stuck in them. Our faith, even our mustard seed sized faith, sustains us so that we can keep pressing our way through. Well, have I got a TESTimony to share with you! As I've heard many times, if you can't say, "Amen!" then say, "Ouch!" So, kick off your shoes, rest in your chaise, grab your cup of coffee or tea and indulge me while I share a few words about perseverance. As I share my testimony, consider your own tests and trials and how they've elevated you and how they've made you a better person. And, if you haven't already done so, we'll work together on how you can share your testimony with other Mothers that may help them as they go through similar situations. Sip, sip and enjoy.

As a pre-teen in the sixth grade, I realized that I had a competitive spirit. I loved tackling new challenges. It gave me the opportunity to learn new things and discover the unimaginable. I didn't necessarily have to win the top prize, per se, but the thought of the grandeur that comes with being number one drove me with fierce determination. If I didn't win the ultimate prize, I was surely going to pursue it with all my might. As I got older, my pursuit to be the lone champion became overshadowed by a sense of team spirit and togetherness. My competitive spirit never lost its zeal, however, I grew more interested in joining forces with others and wanting to accomplish team or family goals rather than viewing everything as "What's in it for me?" I am thankful to God for designing me in such a way as to value my life, as well as the lives of others and all of those nuances that make us unique. For if it had not been for Him protecting me, guiding me, instructing me and loving me throughout the years, I most certainly would've lost my mind. Trust me, there were times, several times, when I really felt like I had come to the end of my rope. I was done. Finished. I would wake up crying, try to piecemeal certain areas of my life to make a story for the day and then fall back asleep crying. I love Psalms 30:5 it says, "Weeping may endure for a night but joy comes in the morning." Sometimes, my mornings wouldn't come for several days, but through pressing and persevering, I eventually found joy and peace again.

To this day, as a wife, working Mother and servant leader, everything I do is for the greater good of the whole rather than apart. I've learned many more valuable lessons when other people were involved. I enjoy gleaning from their experiences as they help in my decision making. Their triumphs and defeats and the stories that make them possible help steer my planning and the decisions I make. My divorce in 2000 was definitely one of those defining moments in my life. No book or words from the wise ever prepared me for that escapade. Some people, especially young people, often tell me how much they wish they could be in my shoes. Well, if they only knew what I've been through, they would, for sure, have second thoughts.

There were problems from the start in our young marriage. Shortly after high school, with about a couple of years of military for my husband and a couple of years of college for me, we decided to get married. We were high school sweethearts whose parents had a combined total of nearly 40 years of marriage at that time. Surely, we would be destined to follow suit after such examples of holy matrimony and "Til death do us part." That belief was true for me, at least, in my fairy tale wanna-be life. My husband, on the other hand, had other plans and decided, not through words, but through his actions, that I was just not enough to keep him satisfied. Perhaps, long-term, in his mind, I would sustain as a dutiful wife, but not without testing and playing in the waters along the way. We moved to California a few months after we got married. My mind told me to stay in Texas in the loving and gentle care of my parents, however, my heart urged me to be with my husband. After all, I needed a full purview of what his life was like without my physical presence. Indeed, I discovered that he had been in a relationship with another woman while we were in our first four months of marriage. Of course, I didn't know that until after I said, "I do." Yes, it was time for me to grow up, move out of the nest and join my husband for a life filled with so-called bliss. Unfortunately, there were so many more bad days than good. I longed to laugh at his jokes again, which had won my heart in the summer of our junior year of high school. He was such a comedian, but jokes during the day and arguments at night became all too familiar. And, suddenly, even his jokes weren't funny anymore. I laughed at them only to keep peace between us, knowing that some flip remark or displeasure in something I had done or not done would come a little later and set the mood for the rest of the evening and even for several days thereafter. It didn't take me long to notice that he intentionally started arguments with me to justify his need to go out and cool off. It was like clockwork. If he wanted to go out, he would ask me a question knowing what my response would be and that would escalate to a full-blown argument. Or, in some cases, he just never came home from work to avoid the argument game altogether. A move back home to Texas in 1992 welcomed more of the same. I cried more and thought more deeply about why I had to go through any of that. I prayed religiously, and others prayed for me and my husband as well. I was mentally and emotionally tormented and drained. After nine years of marital misery, I had enough. When what he had been doing in the dark was revealed in the light, I knew it was time to say good-bye. No one had to tell me the story again and again because I finally saw it for myself. I deserved to be the star of my husband's show, not just a castmate, so we mutually and amicably decided to get a divorce. It was the scariest, most painful thing I had ever endured. It wasn't something that I wanted to do, by any means, but it was something I had to do.

I was happy living the single life, but I wasn't necessarily fulfilled. I enjoyed going out with my girlfriends, and certainly the laughter and sisterhood were great for my sanity. But, going home alone after work or after hanging out with them was not something I looked forward to. I cried often and reflected often on what I could have done differently to save my marriage. I wanted to be in a healthy marriage, but maybe healthy, loving marriages were a thing of the past, something only characterized on TV, I thought. My heart was truly broken. School became a necessity. The routine of going to classes and the homework kept me busy and on the road most evenings after work. Plus, I thoroughly enjoyed the challenge of learning new things and hearing diverse perspectives on different topics. A new world had opened for me, and I found my voice. I spoke up more; I shared ideas more, I offered my opinion more. I stood taller and lifted my head higher, not from pride, but from freedom. The chains had been broken, so I lifted my voice higher and stronger, and I vowed to help women find their own voices, too.

I was in my third session of grad school when my now ex-husband decided to enroll in the same school and prove that he was a changed man. He begged me to give him a second chance, so I did on one condition. He would have to pursue me earnestly as if this was our first time around. We slowly began to date, and eventually we committed ourselves solely to each other. We remarried in 2001. Fast forward to 2017 with two children; I'm in my happy space. This is not at all to say that we haven't had our ups and downs during this second time around, because we have for sure, but we are more mature in our thinking and decision making and we enjoy each other's company. We laugh more. We talk and reflect more. We plan for the future more. We have our moments, like any other marriage, but now our good days outweigh our bad days. We enjoy our marriage enrichment classes at church, and our family ties help keep us stronger. Our children certainly give us a reason to persevere. I truly believe that my testimony of a tumultuous marriage, a divorce and ultimately, a remarriage with my first love, will help someone that's going through a similar experience. Remarriage may not be the solution for everyone. According to USA Today, remarriage rates have dropped nearly 40% in the past 20 years. But, certainly being a determined and dedicated woman who focused on her life has its privileges.

Perseverance is not a word that I use on a regular basis. It is a word, however, that several people have used to describe me. Many stood with me (more like held me up) during my separation and divorce and celebrated with me during our remarriage. I continued my education, enrolling in a Ph.D. program. My mind and body were wired for new learning and discoveries and I was excited to pursue this new challenge. After nine years (something about nine years) and my induction into Phi Kappa Phi, a national honor society, I finally graduated. As were the first two, this graduation was one of the greatest highlights of my life. My sister graduated with her undergraduate degree two days later, so we celebrated all over again. While planning our joint graduation party over the next few weeks, I received a call that would change my life in a huge way.

It was Tuesday, January 14, 2014, my 43rd birthday. I worked from home that day, so that I could go get my driver's license renewed. I wasn't thrilled about taking a new picture for my license since I really liked the last picture I took, which was about eight years prior. About two hours or so into my day, while participating in an online meeting, I received a call from the place where I had recently had my mammogram. I thought nothing of it, in fact, I don't even recall if I looked at my phone initially to see who was calling me. Although I was muted online, I was more interested in not being disruptive during my meeting than trying to figure out who was calling me. I will never forget the next few moments.

I answered the call and the woman on the other end greeted me. She explained to me what company she represented and that she was calling about my recent mammogram and biopsy. There was a short pause and then she asked me if I was sitting down. My conscious left the meeting and I literally looked away from the computer and looked down at my legs before I answered. I confirmed to myself that I was indeed sitting down. I then took a deep breath, closed my eyes and answered her in the affirmative. Then there was a long pause. The representative explained that my biopsy found a small cancer cell in my left breast. Immediately, a single tear rolled down my left eye, followed

32

by a loud gasp. And then, I lost it, but uttered to her, "But, you don't understand. Today is my birthday." I began to sob uncontrollably, trying to catch my breath, but to no avail. If the representative kept talking, I certainly wasn't listening. After several seconds, but still crying and my heart pounding, I managed to sober up a bit to hear her final instructions. "Make an appointment with a breast surgeon as soon as possible," she said in a calm, yet serious manner. The tears flowed non-stop. After our call ended, I sent an instant message to my manager who was still in the meeting. I was brief as I shared with her what was just shared with me. "I have just been diagnosed with cancer....on my birthday." She immediately messaged me back and offered words of comfort, support and encouragement. It meant a great deal to me. I then called my Mother, husband and sister and told them what had just happened. They were very consoling and assured me that everything would be okay. That was enough for me to calm down. I began to pray for strength to get through this. I logged out of my meeting, closed my computer and rested. I sat in my chair in complete silence for several minutes. I prayed some more, then began to ask God, "Why me?" I repeated that question over and over again, even during my ride to the Texas Department of Public Safety. Yes, it was my birthday and of all years, it was time to renew my Driver's License, which meant I had to take a new picture. I was hoping they would allow me to keep my same picture. After all, I looked and felt awful. My eyes were red and swollen from crying so much, not to mention I had an excruciating headache. Surely, they would see I had just experienced a traumatic event and I was not in the mood for pictures, especially a picture that I'd have to keep and display for seven years. Instead, I had to wipe my tears, pull back my hair and attempt to affix a smile on my face worthy for the long term. It was a sad attempt, but I did it.

Immediately after the flash from the camera hit my eyes, I began to cry again. I sobbed and cried ceaselessly and resumed the question, "Why me?" as I returned home. I thought I was living right and treating all people with kindness and respect. I've often heard the question about why do bad things always happen to good people. So, "Why me?" I thought about it and pondered relentlessly about what one incident or event would have caused me to get cancer. I was clueless for nearly an hour as I scoured the medicine cabinet, the refrigerator and pantry, even the water faucet looking for cancer-causing culprits. I had questions, but nothing alarmed me. Then, like a light bulb that suddenly got switched on, it hit me. "Why not me?" That's right! My prayers had been answered.

Several months prior I prayed a very sincere and earnest prayer about my desire to intentionally get closer to God and be a blessing to more people. I felt that I had become disconnected with God. I wasn't spending intimate time with Him and I allowed several other things and people to occupy more of my time, which left only a small window of time to spend in prayer, meditation and studying God's word. And, during that small window, I was always tired and exhausted and rushed through what I felt like were more tasks to check off my daily lists. I was surely not connected. Even during my nightly prayers, I sometimes fell asleep. My prayers were just rote. I truly wanted a closer, more intimate time with God and for Him to enlarge my territory to bless others.

Of course, I didn't know it would be my diagnosis of cancer that would draw me nearer to Him. But, that's exactly what happened. In life, we don't know what circumstances will come our way that will be life changers for us and even our loved ones. When they come, not if, but when, we can't be certain of how long they will last or how intense they will be. It will be to our benefit, perhaps our lifesaver, to be prepared. If we're not prepared and guarded, then anything that comes or blows our way may knock us down and we may not fully recover from that.

I tell my cancer story, not for pity – I did self-pitying enough during the diagnosis and I even continue to have sporadic moments of self-pity – but I tell my story to help others. My blessings come when I encourage others, share resources with others, offer helpful tips to others and connect people to expand their resources. Yes, I have been through a divorce, I have remarried, I have lost loved ones, I have had unplanned (but certainly grateful to have) children, I've been laid off, I've been unemployed for months at a time, I've had to stretch dollars several times, I've been mocked and ridiculed, friends have abandoned me, I could go on and on. I have cried and toiled over each of my previous circumstances, because, quite simply, they hurt and they hurt deeply. My heart has been broken multiple times and there is no way to sugarcoat a broken heart. It is a literal feeling that pieces of your heart have been torn or broken off each time you experience it and each time feels like an eternity.

There is a story to each of those circumstances that have occurred in my life, but I'm thankful that through each one, I've become stronger, more resilient. I realize that everyone's circumstances are different. You, too, have a story to tell. What we go through may not be as deep or traumatic as someone else's or it certainly could be in our minds and based on our backgrounds and lifestyles. The point is that whatever that circumstance or trying situation is, don't wallow in it, prepare your heart and mind for the test and be determined to come out victoriously. And, rest assured that someone else that's going through the same or similar experience could use your listening ear or your helpful advice on how you've made it. Your tests will become your testimonies, your trials will become your triumphs and your setbacks will become your comebacks. The following is my all-time, tried and true formula to help you persevere through your circumstances.

 FAITH

At the very foundation of any of our circumstances should be our faith in something greater than ourselves. My faith in God kept me during my darkest days and my faith is what continues to keep me humbled and secure during waves of calmness and turbulence. My faith certainly assured me, even at my weakest points, that somehow, some way I would survive and make it through another day. It gave me hope, a brighter outlook and a positive perspective in the midst of constant change. In addition to my faith, I also had the courage to seek professional counseling when I needed it. There is nothing shameful about seeking professional counseling. Faith without works is dead. I do believe that prayer works, but it takes faith and action for change to happen. With counseling, I was able to talk openly about my situations without being judged and I learned key strategies for how to deal with them in a healthy and manageable way.

One of those healthy ways was forgiveness. Forgiveness is still a struggle for me at times. Movie scenes, clichés, song lyrics, a familiar argument, you name it, will trigger past events that make it difficult for me to move on. Even when my husband and I are having a relatively good day, sometimes several consecutive days, something will cross my mind or cross my line of sight that will cause me to remember a horrible time in my past and revert to harbored related feelings. Because of many lessons on faith and forgiveness, these feelings are like vapors; they're there, but for a minute. In the past, I would let these renewed negative feelings take advantage of me and pull me into a state of instant depression that would last for several days. At that time, I certainly didn't look like what I had been through. I was able to mask and hide my feelings very well, especially from my children. I was so determined not to allow what I was experiencing to impact my children in any way, or so I thought. I've learned that children have a keen sense of what their parents are going through. And my daughter, for sure, who would often ask me in her sweet, quiet voice, as she still does today, "Mom, are you okay? What's wrong? Are you sure nothing's wrong? You can tell me. Please, Mommy." I would hold in my feelings as best as I could and always answer, "I'm fine baby girl. Don't worry about me." Forgiveness truly does free you and I'm so glad that it's a priority goal for me.

FAMILY

There were many times during my challenges that I felt like I was alone. I was too embarrassed to share my pain with others, including my family members. I'm sure they didn't realize that the many times I called when I said I just called to say hello or to see how they were doing that I really was calling to get comfort from the sheer mention of "Hi Mama" or "Hey Sis."Just their verbal acknowledgment was enough to give me a sense of peace. I could not explain what I was going through, not even a hint, because my pain was too deep. I also didn't want them to bear my pain because they had their own circumstances to deal with. Hearing the voices and laughter of my family members soothed and coaxed me to get through the day or night. I tell you, there is nothing like family. I certainly appreciate mine. They have been and continue to be my rock. They're my babysitters, my chauffeurs, my meal providers, my chat and chew buddies, my co-mourners, my after school and after game picker-uppers, my cheerleaders, my PTA meetings and events stand-ins, my party planners, my on-call hairstylists, my lawn care providers.... they're my everything. I truly could not be where I am today, mind, body and spirit, without each of them. When you've got family, you've got the whole world, so take care of them and appreciate them.

⏻ FOCUS

For every type of relationship that we initiate and build, I learned two very profound questions that we should ask ourselves in this order, 1) "Where am I going?" and 2) "Who's going with me?". I remember sitting in my Research Methods class in grad school and my professor shared those two questions with us. At the time, I was going through the final stage of my divorce and for whatever reason, she prefaced her lecture that evening with those questions, they hit me like a ton of bricks. "Wow!" I thought. My goals that I have set for myself and my personal values should not be altered or canceled by anyone but me. But, here's the caveat, those two questions must be asked and answered in that same order. You can't play switcharoo with these two questions. If you have hopes, dreams and plans of going to college, changing careers, getting a makeover, joining a club or association, starting a new business, or whatever, then you've answered the first question. Those that support you, such as your family, friends and colleagues answer the second question. If you change the sequence of these two questions, then your goals are not your own, they are someone else's. Of course, it's so much easier to ask these two questions before you become attached to someone or accept a new job. However, if you find yourself becoming frustrated and you feel like you're being pulled in two or more directions, refocus and ask yourself those two basic questions again. What you ultimately decide to do is up to you. Throughout my tests, I've asked myself those two questions and the revelations were never surprising. I have no regrets about my life's circumstances, only life lessons. Only God knows what would have become had I asked those two questions much earlier in my life.

⏻ FORTITUDE

My former First Lady at my church, who is now deceased, often advised the women of our church to put on our "big girl's panties." It took me awhile to understand what she meant. Often when we go through our tests and trials, we may feel like we're getting weaker. It's because the weight of the burdens feel way too heavy to bear and we feel like the odds are too much against us. In our minds, and because of the physical tolls on our bodies, we think we are weak and vulnerable. However, if we prepare our hearts and minds for spiritual warfare and are steadfast through the war, then we will come out with victory.

When I got laid off from my job, I was devastated. I loved the work I did, I enjoyed the benefits and perks and the company was one of the top five in its industry. I loved my job so much I had planned to retire from the company. I continued my graduate education twice to remain in my chosen field and I carefully sought my employer. So, when the chatter got louder about possible layoffs, especially in my division, I began to casually scout prospective employers. Still, I refused to fully embrace the thought that my job would end soon. Thankfully, I received my notice in January for the March layoff, which gave me about two months to prepare for this life-altering event.

Things were going great for the first few weeks following the layoff. The severance was enough to help pay the bills through the end of April and after a couple of weeks, my unemployment benefits kicked in to help supplement our living expenses and incidentals. I had intensified my job search by updating my LinkedIn profile, creating several more revisions to my resume – one for each type of job or industry that I was open to. I felt very optimistic about my prospects. For sure, my education and all those years of professional experience would pay off. I would surely land my dream job soon.

My days became longer and my weeks even longer. My phone didn't ring. My inbox was filling up with advertisements and meeting notices, but nothing came from companies that I had applied to. Nothing. It would be a month before I got my first phone interview. That ended up going nowhere. It would be nearly three weeks later before I would get another phone interview and the next one came two weeks later. My first in-person interview came almost three months after I was laid off. I began to seriously worry. I also began to self-doubt my skills and abilities. Perhaps, I thought, I should minimize my education and some of my experience on my resume to look more appealing, less qualified and less intimidating. Or, maybe I should apply for entry-level positions and not the senior level or leadership positions that were more aligned with my experience. It became a constant battle as I decided to widen my scope and apply for all experience and educational levels. As I reviewed the pages and pages of entries that I had for completed job applications, phone screenings and phone and in-person interviews, I was both amazed and disheartened that the total number had topped 150 in just a seven-week period, most of which were applications and only a handful were interviewed. I often prayed, even though it hurt so badly to do so. I'm so thankful to my family and close friends who encouraged me and prayed for and with me during that time.

Finally, through a trusted colleague who put in a good word for me, both verbally and on paper, I got a call for an interview that I felt was the most promising of all the previous ones. The role was exactly what I wanted to do and what I could do. It was a perfect match. Then, several weeks later, I got a call for a second interview, which included a presentation. I nailed it! Subsequently, I received a job offer, accepted the offer and started my new job less than two weeks later. Consequently, on my first day at work, I also learned that I had exhausted my unemployment benefits just a few days prior. Right at the moment when the unemployment representative shared the final date of payment, I dropped the phone, lowered my head, tears streaming, then I raised my head and said, "Thank you, Jesus! Only You, God."

⏻ FUN

Celebrate small wins. I betcha I can count on one hand the number of times that I've had a massage or treated myself (and only myself) to a fancy dinner or even just had one full day to myself (and only myself). It's rare. I would even take one hour in the day! I've adapted to celebrating with others, allowing them to join in on my fun for every

The Face of Perseverance

occasion. I've always thought, the more, the merrier. I can only imagine what it's like, as I've heard from a few Moms, to book a night or two at a nearby hotel, order room service, work out for an hour or so, take a swim and just lay back and relax – all by myself (and only myself!). That day is coming because as I get older, I realize that I deserve to celebrate my accomplishments in my own way. It's not that I want to be selfish, but for the sake of my sanity, I must celebrate the baby steps in my life.

With the right tools and resources, you can beat the odds, accomplish your goals and live a very fulfilling life. When I decided to run for a public office, I did so with a focus on improving the educational needs and lives of the students in my school district, as well as enhancing the communities in which our students reside. My win for my first elected position as a board trustee was because of sheer determination, sacrifices and a selfless desire to serve others in a way that positively impacts their lives forever. Through the years, I've had ups and downs and life has surely thrown some curve balls my way. It hasn't been easy to get up after falling or heal after being broken so many times. But, thankfully, I can lift my head, smile and reflect on so many good things that I've been blessed with. My balance is knowing that my husband (honey-do), my children, my parents, my sister and the rest of my family and friends are the most loving and supportive human beings in my life, that my work (on and off the clock) is meaningful and that God is my ultimate Rock!!

"From everyone who has been given much, much will be demanded; and from the one who has been entrusted with much, much more will be asked." Luke 12:48

Where do you find your POWER?

The birth of my oldest daughter taught me how to be strong. I now have three children and each child motivates me in their own way to push forward in life. They all have their own personalities and I feel my job is to set the best example as a woman, wife, and mother to them as I can. I feel if I set the standards they will set out to go above and beyond to exceed them. I also like to motivate and inspire people. When someone tells me that I have motivated them or inspired them to do something I tend to draw from that. That feeling that I have helped someone makes me want to help as many people that I can to step out of their comfort zone and go after their dreams.

Chapter 3

Re-Discover Your Self-Identity

"What lies behind us and what lies before us are tiny matters compared to what lies within us".
Ralph Waldo Emerson

It's a natural reaction to be self-conscious of how other people may perceive you. After all, society keeps us cognizant of what's "socially acceptable"; setting the standard on how one should look, dress, and even who we should have within our circles. We unknowingly become persuaded and pressured to pretend to be something we're not, just to fit in a crowd. I felt the effects of this at a very young age.

I was emotionally scarred as a child, by the way the other kids treated me. I endured the stares, the laughter, the picking on by other kids; just because of my appearance. Growing up I had many external flaws that I was ashamed of, and unfortunately, I couldn't do anything to correct them. I was a fair-skinned little girl who developed Vitiligo (a disease that destroys the pigment cells of the skin), at an early age. Essentially, I had light patches on different areas of my face.

I also wore thick glasses that magnified my eyes, and I had crowded teeth. I was a true sweetheart, but of course the other kids couldn't see that. I could almost hear their thoughts out loud, Why did she wear that? What's that on her face? Why are her glasses so big? I dealt with them picking on me and calling me names during a lot of my youth. I hoped one day they could see the "real" me, past all my blemishes and imperfections.

Things started to change a bit as I entered eighth grade. I was able to cover up my external flaws by wearing light makeup to cover the patches, changing my glasses to contacts, and eventually getting braces. I started putting more time and effort into my outward appearance. I was considered somewhat of a pretty good dresser, so I played to that strength. I hoped that by making these outward changes, people would see me differently, and wouldn't judge me as much. But, even after making these changes I was still self-conscious. I was afraid to go places alone, and I would still sit quietly in the back of the room. I was terrified to attend events. No matter whether I was alone or in a group, I had convinced myself the people were judging me the minute I walked in. It always felt like all eyes were on me. I didn't feel as if they were looking at me to welcome me either, but, I felt like the looks were always very judgmental, picking me apart from head to toe. As a self-defensive mechanism, I remembered I would always sit towards the back of the room and be as quiet as a church mouse. I was scared that if I made the slightest move, it would draw unwanted attention to myself, so I made sure to tiptoe around people. In my mind, the less attention brought to me the less people would focus on my external flaws.

When it came to my home life, I was also somewhat of a people pleaser in my younger days. Like most children, I always wanted to make sure I was doing right in the eyes of my grandparents, parents; setting an example for my sister. Growing up I was taught to graduate high school, go to college, get a job, get married, and have a family. That was the American Dream or at least that's what I was taught. I completed the first step by graduating high school but then my life plans were altered after that. Instead of going to college, I headed to join the workforce and I landed a decent paying job for someone straight out of high school, with no college degree.

It was during that time that I met my husband, Adrian. We dated, and during the interim, I became pregnant with my oldest daughter. Three years after my high school graduation my daughter made her entrance into the world. It was a little scary; she arrived 15 weeks early and had to stay in the hospital months after she was born. It was totally unexpected, but I made the adjustment quickly, to becoming a mother to an underweight preemie. Those first months were tough, as the doctors didn't expect her to survive. I knew different. I felt in my spirit that she was a fighter just like her mommy. Adrian was still in college for another year before he graduated. Once he graduated, I went on to pursue my Associate's degree and shortly after my Bachelor's. In my eyes, our daughter would have two parents to look up to with educational degrees. We wanted to set the standard for her level of education. We went on to marry while I was pursuing my education. Six years later we welcomed our second daughter and a little over a year after that our son arrived. Our family was growing rapidly.

Things had started changing for me. As a woman, I was more self-aware of who I was becoming. Motherhood had attributed to my maturity and my outlook on life. Work was consistent for me, and by this time, I was approaching 12 years with the same company. I had changed departments a few times within the company, but I always had my mind set on advancing my career and becoming a buyer. It wasn't until I was placed in a position, that I knew could help me get closer to becoming a buyer, that I started having thoughts about whether being a buyer was actually for me... Maybe the grass wasn't greener on the other side. The opportunities to climb the corporate ladder were there. However; those opportunities were being presented to people coming in from the outside more so than to those on the inside. I knew I wasn't being overlooked due to a lack of experience or skills. At the time, I was working directly with an executive buyer, and in a lot of situations, I made executive decisions on her behalf. My year-end accomplishments spoke for itself, so there was truly no legitimate reason for me not being promoted or at least placed into the entry-level program. Even with my experience and accomplishments, year after year, I received broken promises from the company. I finally decided to acquire additional experience in another area that would hopefully bring me back to a buying position.

After 4 years in the next position my spirit changed, my outlook changed, my attitude changed, and my wants changed. I began to take a deeper look at who I was and what I really wanted out of my life. I grew tired of going to work every day doing the same routine over and over. I know you are probably thinking who doesn't get tired of going to work? I get it, and I get that we must go to work to make money and pay the bills. Trust me; I understand all of that. I was no stranger to working, I started working my first job at 14. However, I was almost to the point of being miserable. I started coming in to work later and later. I did my job, but with no passion for it. I placed minimal effort in completing my day-to-day task. At this point I was clear. I had discovered that it was no longer a desire of mine to grow within the company. I was unhappy with myself as a woman, mother, and wife. I felt that I owed so much more to myself and my family, but I couldn't figure out what I was lacking or what I was yearning for.

During this time, the company was trying to cut back, and buyouts were being offered. Buyouts had been offered twice previously and it never occurred to me during the first two times, that it could be an option for me to make a move. However, after the second one, I started to think about the pros and cons of me taking it, if they offered it again. I originally talked the decision over with my husband and a close friend. I decided to pray about it and if the buyout was offered again, I would apply. My only concern was whether the terms would meet my financial expectations. To my surprise, the buyout was offered again! I was faced with a crossroads. It was time for me to make a decision. I had to ask myself what I really wanted for myself and out of life. I knew that I no longer wanted to be a buyer for the company. I also knew that I no longer wanted to get up and work on someone else's schedule or better yet for someone else. I realized I still wanted to be a buyer but not for an employer. I really wanted to be a buyer for my own business. I have always had a love for fashion and the idea of me buying for my own boutique excited me.

I applied for the buyout with only a few people knowing. When it was approved, I met with HR and they showed me what I would leave with financially. The numbers were what I expected, so I took that as God's confirmation and I signed my papers. The question now was what would be my next move and what steps would I be willing to take to get there. I knew in order for me to answer that question, I would have to take a deep look into myself and do an even deeper self-evaluation. Even though I had the support of my husband and my family, this would ultimately affect our household. I could not set goals or plan my next move until I was comfortable with knowing me as a person and understanding my expectations for myself. I had to determine who Jaquithia Stinson really was and what she truly wanted to achieve. Ultimately, I had to examine myself from the inside out as a woman, mother, wife, friend, and business owner. In other words, I had to re-discover my true identity.

Before I left the company, I was off to a good start with some of the preliminary tasks that comes with starting a business. I came up with the name, business plan, and registered with all necessary legal parties. By this time everyone that I associated with at work knew I was leaving. I had the support of quite a few people. For all of those people that offered support I humbly accepted every encouraging word, prayer, or suggestion. As you know in most situations with good comes some bad. I heard the views of people that really couldn't understand why I was making such a big decision at such a young age. I was told how I would lose seniority with the company and how I wouldn't be able to take another federal job for five years. I was asked questions like, "What about your benefits? and What will you do for retirement?"

Several people didn't believe in me and what I was setting out to do with my boutique. I was told, you have a husband and three children to take care of and now you are going to put all the financial weight on him? Yes, that was one of the many questions asked from people on the outside looking in. In all honesty, it was a valid concern, but it wasn't anyone else's business. What they didn't know is that I had his full support and I still do. A lot of times people tend to criticize what they don't understand. Sometimes they bash it because they don't have the courage to do it themselves. Either way, that wasn't weight for me to carry. I realized that in life your mission is to stick to your goals and not compromise yourself or your plan for anything or anyone. Remember what is given by God cannot be destroyed by man and this includes your goals and aspirations. I prayed to God about my decision and He gave me peace and confirmation, and I did not need man's approval. And while I realized that some people sincerely wanted to make sure my family would be ok with such a major transition, and they had valid questions for me to consider, I was at peace knowing that I was making the right decision. I put myself in a position to move forward with my plans. I've always been a person that made big decisions and didn't look back. I believe in living life with no regrets. I do not make decisions expecting to fail, however, if I do fail, I know I'll be okay. You may feel that's an odd way of thinking since nothing in life is for sure. I look at things from the point of, if I never try it I would never know if I would fail or succeed. I'd rather step out on faith and test the waters then spend time wondering or singing the old should've, would've, could've song that's sung by so many living life with regrets. Life is about chances. You can't always play it safe. Sometimes you have to take the chance and either succeed or fail. Just know that if you fail, you must bounce back. The key is not to let anything hold you down or keep you from at least attempting to achieve your dreams.

Before I made this leap, I needed to be in tuned and at peace with me. I had to learn my true personality. I had to understand who I really was when it was just me alone. Not the person that wears ten hats but who I was without the hats. I had to get in touch with what I really liked and disliked. I had to evaluate my triggers, and understand why those things triggered me. I had to learn why I reacted a certain way to things. For example, I'm big on customer service. If the customer service in a store or restaurant is not to my standards, it really bothers me. If it's horrible, I will personally speak with the manager or maybe even write a review. I may give the establishment a second try depending on how horrible the first experience was. However, the second experience must be almost over the top for me to make a third visit. Why is that? I thought long and hard about that at first. Then I remembered that my first full-time job was in customer service. It taught me how to provide great customer service. Therefore, it also taught me what to expect when I was on the other end. I look at customer service as treating people how you would want to be treated. Therefore, you wouldn't want me to serve you with an attitude so don't do it to me.

While doing my self-evaluation, I also realized that I'm also a person that doesn't like to be told that I can't do something within the proper boundaries. I have to try it and prove that I can do it or learn the reasons why it can't be done versus someone telling me I can't and I just concede, with no questions asked. Something doesn't sit right with me when a person tells me what I can't do if I haven't been given a fair opportunity to at least try. With that in mind, I would say settling is not a personality trait that I carry. It's important for everyone to understand their own personality. Understanding and acknowledging your personality will come in handy when dealing with other people. You may be able to recognize traits of someone you are looking to do business with or even starting a relationship with that may clash with yours. Understanding your personality gives you a sense of if the person or situation is something suitable for you. With that in mind, you can determine whether you should embrace a situation or block it. I looked at myself in a few areas that were helpful in my discovering my true self.

I can remember when I was working on a big project and there was a team of people assisting me with the project. One person played more of a major part in the initial development of the project than the others. With that said that person became a very valuable player on the team and at lot depended on him. As the deadline was approaching, I started seeing a lapse in the communication with this teammate. I am what you may call a very detailed person. If I'm working on a project and I need information I like to hear the in-depth report and not a summary. As we started to approach our deadlines, I started asking for information that I need to relay to other team members. The team lead wasn't giving me thoroughly detailed information; I kept receiving a summary of the information. Because of my personality, my initial reaction was to try and eliminate any unnecessary stress from both sides, so we could move forward and complete the project. However, what I truly meant for good was mistaken as me being unprofessional, pushy, and controlling. I was baffled by the response, and I was a little hurt by how things started going south, when in my mind, I was trying to be helpful so we could complete the project. One of my teammates pointed out some things to me about my personality. They emphasized things that I had always considered a good trait of mine, but in that situation, it was misunderstood. I conducted an inner reflection on what I had done to contribute to the misunderstanding. I was able to see things from all parties involved and make the necessary adjustments. Since then I have come to understand my personality, and I have learned how to try and adapt to others when it's necessary. Everyone cannot handle a strong personality. I will never change who I am, but I can adapt and "tone down" when necessary, to achieve the greater good.

⏻ Connect with your Core Values

I also evaluated myself from a moral standpoint. I asked myself, "What do I consider my core values to be?" Core values to me are the things that I hold close to my heart; they are my personal convictions that I abide by, no matter what. My most important values consist of my faith, loyalty, respect, love, and honesty. Everyone should have a moral reflection. When you do, you should determine your core values, you should think of what's important to you. When you live your life with these values in mind, it makes it easier to make decisions when placed in uncomfortable situations. When I knew in my heart and spirit that it was time for me to make a change in my career, I believed that my faith would carry me during the transition. Faith can take you places that man can't and take you to places that you couldn't imagine. The compassion, respect, and love that I have for others create connections. Being transparent or honest shows people that I'm human just as they are, and that enables me to connect with people that I need.

Everyone will not see your vision. However, it's up to you to stay true to yourself and not stray from your beliefs. In continuing with becoming in tune with myself, I also identified my likes and dislikes. This goes back to being true to myself.

I questioned whether I was a person that liked fads or if I liked things because of its authenticity and creativeness? I've never been into name brands. I feel if it's something that catches my eye then it's something worth me taking a gander at regardless of what someone else may think. Staying true to yourself and what interest you will help you to be the best you. When you stay true to your feelings, you don't spend time trying to please everyone else. It's okay not to like everything that your girlfriend likes. You may have different taste in things like fashion or even men. That doesn't mean you aren't meant to be friends. It simply means you have your own taste in what you like. In a lot of friendships and relationships that may be the glue that holds your relationship together. Sometimes you need to be around people that balance you. You don't need a bobblehead, which I refer to as a "yes" person. Most of the time the person that tells you yes to everything is not in your life for your best interest. You want to surround yourself with people that will be honest with you at all times.

⏻ Love Yourself

Accepting yourself means being comfortable and loving every aspect of you. I struggled with my weight from my 20's, and I am still conscious of it today. However, what I can say is at whatever weight I am, I own it. I have never considered myself a "brick house," I'm more so cute in the face and thick in the waist. Society has set so many standards that they apply across the board for everyone. I am not thin, and I am comfortable with that. Everyone is not built or wired the same. We have to stop comparing ourselves to other women. You should always have confidence in who you are, the way God made you. By no means am I a conceited person, but I am comfortable enough with me now. I can walk in a room full of the most beautiful and well-proportioned women and not feel an ounce of intimidation. That's not something that I have always been able to say. The truth is that I endured a lot of hurt and pain before I got to this point of confidence. However, once I did realize my worth, I decided there was no one or situation that could make me doubt it again. As you grow older your body changes, your features change, and even your hair changes. The thing is that we can't stop the inevitable, but we can embrace it. GOD made us perfectly and uniquely in His image. While it took me some time to see that, I now understand and love who I am both inside and out. I also appreciate the periods in my life when I went through the hurt and pain as it strengthened me. I understand that I'm not 25 anymore so I don't expect for my body to look like a 25-year-old either. However, I like to compare aging with wine and I do believe I have gotten better with time. Some of us are naturally fit and others (me) have to work at it. As we age the more we must invest in our mental and physical health. I understand that life can be so overwhelming at times, but we won't have a life to live if we don't invest in taking care of ourselves both mentally and physically.

As my 38th birthday was approaching, I made a promise to myself to get in the gym or at least get in some exercise as much as possible. Now, I have a husband, three active kids, and a dog; my life is very lively. However, taking time for me to invest in my health has really made a difference in my days. For the most part I work out in the mornings, and it has truly helped me in respects to my mood and concentration level throughout the day. The big plus is I've lost some weight too! Exercising is an additional step I took towards working on a better me. One thing that I have always been very passionate about as a woman is making time for myself.

Although I love being a mother, wife, and entrepreneur, I've learned that my life cannot be solely about my family and business. Every woman needs to have her "me time". It can be time spent getting pampered, journaling, or time spent meditating in thoughts. It most definitely can be time spent with your girls. However, you decide to get in your "me time" the goal should be to unwind and just enjoy the moment. I make it my mission to get my time in once or twice a month. Sometimes it could be more than that if the opportunity presents itself. I consider it a way to regroup or recharge yourself. After you've had that time to yourself, you are ready to handle the next thing life throws at you. Essentially, you can't give the best of yourself to your family, friends, or any business if you are not taking steps to take care of yourself.

⏻ Clarity of the Vision

As I was discovering my true self-identity, I wrote out my dreams and aspirations. Being able to understand my dreams and aspirations helped me to develop a plan to make them into reality. I reached a point where I didn't want HR to determine how I could dress at work, when I could retire, what I would retire with, and how my life would be set-up after retirement. I decided I wanted to control my future by creating my own path to a happy life. Following my dreams meant I could live a life that I planned for myself, a life I would be proud to live and a legacy I could leave behind for my children.

I want to challenge you to get in touch with your true self-identity and go after your dreams. Following your dreams means that you understand things will not come easy. In fact, most of the time things get harder, especially if it's something blessed by God. However, you must be up to the challenge to get to where you want to be. There is much more gratification in accomplishing something that you worked for and own than something that came easy and doesn't benefit you. There is always a chance of failing but just like we tell the kids when riding their bikes, you have to get back up and try it again. You may have to readjust some things the next go around, but quitting is never an option. Going after your dreams takes faith, strength, persistence, and determination. With those attributes in mind, the obstacles will come but you will be better equipped to handle them. Surround yourself with likeminded people. Not yes, people but people that are trying to elevate. Again, when you are trying to take yourself to the next level, you should only want to bring those with you that will support and encourage you along the way. The unfortunate truth about that is everyone will not travel to the next level with you.

I'm a firm believer that people come into your life for reasons and seasons. When you learn to accept that some people have fulfilled their purpose in your life, it's easier to let go when you need to. I have dealt with the fake friends along this journey, and I know how upsetting that can be. Most of my life I was around fake friends. You know the ones that love you to death until they see you are doing something that may take you to the next level. This was also part of my battle within myself. I always aimed to be the friend that I would want anyone to be to me, but unfortunately it wasn't reciprocated. In most situations, I would end up questioning who I was as a person. I wondered if I was truly the person that I thought I was to others. I had to learn that with elevation comes separation.

While working on getting to know me, one of the things I realized was that I had to learn how to tune people out that didn't support my vision. I had to separate myself from people that were not around me to motivate me. I understand what may be for me will not be for everyone. My thought is you don't have to love it but please respect my vision or there's no reason for us to be associated with each other. Anyone that truly knows me as a person knows that I'm all about motivating and uplifting people to achieve their dreams.

⏻ Keep Dreaming…Keep Moving

Dreams can be accomplished at any age and you don't need a gang load of people to make it happen. I have a 10-year-old daughter with a nonprofit organization. I left a job of 15 years to start my fashion boutique at age 35. Nothing is impossible. You are the only person that can stand in the way of you achieving your goals. You must believe in yourself and go after what you want. Prayer is a must and your faith must be strong. Those two components alone will carry you to depths far beyond your belief.

Before I decided to become a business owner, I asked myself a few questions. Did I want to continue waking up and going to a job that I really didn't have a passion for? If I stayed would I be living up to my full potential? Was I ready for this challenge? Can I handle what will come with being an entrepreneur? Do I have the knowledge and skills that it will take to be successful? Was this really what I wanted, or did I just need a change of scenery? While all those questions came to mind, they could only be answered after I conducted my self-evaluation. Now you must think about what questions you need to ask yourself to make sure you are in touch with yourself, and with your true self-identity. When you know who you are you can determine what you really want. From that point, all that is left is for you to go after it and make your dreams a reality. I continue to enjoy this journey life has taken me on. I want to encourage you to get to know your true self. It's a feeling of freedom when you understand who you really are as a person.

Meet Shantania Leggins

Where do you find your POWER?

As you will read in my chapter, I have seen my share of challenges. What keeps me going and keeps me centered is my Faith in God. Nothing more, nothing less. Despite of me, I believe God truly loves me and created me to impact this world for generations. I whole hardheartedly believe this, and this is what I stand on daily. My POWER is connected to my Faith.

Chapter 4

Financially Empowered Moms Leave a Legacy

"You Can Have It All, Just Not All at Once"

Oprah Winfrey

"You Can Have It All, Just Not All at Once" is a quote I heard years ago. I was in my early twenties when I heard one of my mentors say it, and it has stuck with me to this day. When I first heard it, I must admit, it didn't make a lot of sense to me. As I continued to ponder it, the only situation that came to mind that this would apply, or even make sense would be a buffet line. I chuckle, as I am a brown girl from down south who loves to cook and eat, so relating things to food is a common occurrence for me. So much so, that in many of my circles, I am known as a food connoisseur. As years passed, I continued to assume this was the meaning of this saying - I eventually had an aha moment! After being married a couple of years, having a couple of kids and taking a stab at entrepreneurship - all while working a corporate job - I heard the quote again, "You can have it all, just not all at once." At that moment the light bulb went off. I finally understood what that quote meant.

Life is full of tradeoffs and at different phases in your life, the "it" changes. You can have it all, but not all at once. At 22, I was newly married with a kid and lots of energy, hopes, and dreams. Sixteen years later, I am still married, now with 5 kids, a little less energy, but still many hopes and dreams and a lot more living to do. Having it all at 22 with one kid, working in corporate America looks different from how I define having it all now. I am a huge believer that there is nothing you cannot do, be or have. What I now know is that you may not be able to do, be and have it all at the same time. "You Can Have It All Just Not All at Once."

One of the challenges with a buffet line, as in life, is our eyes tend to be bigger than our stomachs. When you first get to a buffet line, it's easy just to dive in and get carried away. In life, we sometimes want what we want, when we want it, without giving thought to or questioning is this the right thing and if it is the right time? That is a recipe for disaster! Diving into anything without knowing the full extent of what you're up against isn't just a poor strategy for buffets, it's a poor strategy for life.

Prepared or not, life happens to the best of us. Despite having grown up without much materially, despite my parents' financial mistakes, I somehow found myself doing OK financially as a very young adult. My mother wanted to ensure we did not repeat some of her money mistakes, so she constantly shared many of them and encouraged us to save, save, save. At the time, I had no formal knowledge about finances; I was just being obedient. In 2001, I was married with a kid and by 26 we were parents of two. During that time, I had worked for what was then a Big 5 accounting firm and spent a few years at the only fortune 500 company in Louisiana. By most standards, for a couple under 30, we were doing pretty well. Let's call that period, the calm before the storm – literally.

In August of 2005, we experienced one of the largest natural disasters to hit the US - Hurricane Katrina. The storm would permanently displace us from our home, our city and our entire life as we knew it. This was a defining moment! My husband and I, along with our two young kids who were 4 years old and 11 months at the time, went from being homeowners to homeless in a matter of a day. During this tragedy, not knowing it at the time, I would have my first A.S.S.E.S.S the situation moment. I will expound on that later. In the days after Katrina, like most, we had no idea what was next. We didn't know if we still had jobs, if we still had our home or when could we go back to our city. There were so many what-ifs. After evacuating to Arkansas and spending a couple of weeks there, we would eventually find ourselves in Houston, TX. While we were both given the opportunity to return to our jobs, due to all of the uncertainties and unknowns during this time, we made the illogical decision to begin our pursuit of full-time entrepreneurship. While these were uncertain and devastating times, because we had practiced some of the principles and concepts discussed later in this chapter we were able to bounce back and begin to rebuild our lives in a new city.

I wish I could say this was the last storm I would encounter. In the summer of 2006, we built a home in a suburb outside of Houston and were beginning to create a new normal. Life would happen again. In Fall of 2007, my mother, the matriarch of our family who also relocated to Houston suffered a brain aneurysm. It burst and required brain surgery. During this time, I realized Katrina had only been preparation for dealing with the uncertainty of life - yet again. Nonetheless, nothing compares to the thought of losing your mother, so I thought. By the Grace of God, she survived, but would now need help more than ever. Again, because we had practiced many of the concepts mentioned later in the chapter and now I was a full-time entrepreneur, I had the time and resources to support her as needed. Life would continue on and in 2008 we had child # 3. On June 16, 2011, we were blessed yet again with child # 4. This one was sweet! We finally had our two boys (KJ and Kayden) and our two girls (Kennedy and Kassidy). Who said God doesn't give you more than you can bear?

On June 17th we brought child #4 home from the hospital. He was a beautiful, bouncing, healthy baby boy! The very next morning would change EVERYTHING! I woke up to change and nurse our new bundle only to find him unresponsive. On June 18, 2011, our sweet Kayden Addison was pronounced dead. To make matters worse, his death was attributed to SIDS, which means they never found a real cause of death. This storm would stop us in our tracks – mentally, physically, emotionally, spiritually and financially. I know without a shadow of a doubt, nothing compares to losing your child. Nothing! Six years later, I know God had begun preparing us for this one too as we dealt with our other storms. While

66

having practiced the concepts mention later in the chapter helped us get back on track and I am sure softened some of the blows - we felt this one financially. At this point, we were both full-time entrepreneurs and had begun building a business. The loss of a kid takes your breath, so we pressed the pause button on many of our business operations. Many of the partners we had at the time quit and left us pretty much just with each other. Eventually, we were able to pick up the pieces and get back moving again.

I share these stories with you because life happens to the best of us, prepared or not. Each of these tragic events could have knocked us out cold, But God! You can't go back and change the past, but you can start right now and change your future. Despite what you have done in the past financially, the financial choices and decisions you make now will determine how you can respond when life happens or for some, when it happens again. If you are married, single, with kids or without, this chapter is for you. You will gain insight into what it takes to begin building or rebuilding financially.

If life has you on your second go 'round in some areas or perhaps you are still in line for your first serving, the next few pages in this chapter are going to be all about how to A.S.S.E.S.S. the situation and become a Financially Empowered MOM who Leaves a Legacy of Faith and Finances.

⏻ A.S.S.E.S.S. the Situation

Assess means to evaluate or estimate the nature, ability, or quality of; calculate or estimate the price or value of; set the value of. Life is a journey and sometimes we can get stuck in the same position for a long time or we may even get lost. There are times when we may get frustrated by our lack of progress financially and even in other areas of our lives. This is when we need to stop and take the time to A.S.S.E.S.S our situation. We need to look at where we are now, where we want to go, and how we intend to get there. This chapter is all about becoming a financially empowered mom, so our time together will be centered on the financial part of life.

⏻ Attitude Check

Money speaks one language… If you save me today I will save you tomorrow! The first step in assessing the situation is to do an attitude check. Repeat after me. "Attitude is 100% of everything (we will prove it later in the chapter). My attitude about my finances matter". If you're feeling overwhelmed and discouraged about your finances, one of the most important things you can do to change your financial life, is change your attitude about it. Remember the adage, "your attitude determines your altitude." We all have beliefs and attitudes about everything of importance to us: religion, kids, politics, fashion, etc. We also have an attitude about money. Your money attitude is your belief about money. Your attitude about money defines everything that matters about your personal financial situation. How much money do you need? How hard are you willing to work for it? What does money mean to you, what does it represent? How do you feel about money? How much does money influence your non-financial decisions? Your money attitude is your way of thinking about money. Your beliefs become your attitude and your attitude influence your words and actions.

What's your attitude about money? Money attitudes are shaped by our childhood experiences, and family plays a big part in giving us money lessons. Whether good or bad, how you handle money as an adult stems from how those around you in your childhood handled money. You either learn what to do or what not to do. In many ways, the age-old saying, "like mother, like daughter" rings true for many of our attitudes toward personal finances. Your family's socioeconomic status can have an important effect on your cognitive skills and socio-emotional development, which in turn affects your attitude toward money. If we want to be financially empowered moms we must check our attitudes about money as WE WILL play an integral part in shaping our kids' attitudes about money.

A - 1

T -20

T - 20

I – 9

T – 20

U – 21

D – 4

E – 5

*Attitude is 100% of Everything

*Each letter is assigned the value of where it falls in the alphabets. Ex. A is the 1st letter and E is the 5th letter

*70 to 80 percent of women will be solely in control of their finances at some point, either because they marry later or never, divorce, or end up widowed. This is why you need to seize control of your financial life. When you seize something, you take hold of it quickly, firmly, and forcefully. Ladies, this is the approach you need with your finances. How do you do this? It starts with purging your mind of the traditional social views like, "women aren't wired for financial matters." Regardless of what "they" say, make a decision to learn how money works. Accept that it may require you to fall in love with reading and learning how to play the money game. You may have to trade off the next fashion show for the upcoming financial workshop. The most important thing to do is to decide that you are going to take control of your finances - then take action.

Repeat after me, "A Man is NOT a Plan!" one more time "A Man is NOT a Plan!" Do not misinterpret this message, seizing control of your finances and becoming financially empowered doesn't mean you have to separate your money from your spouse. However, it does mean you need to be a part of the planning process. If you have a spouse, you should be knowledgeable about the family's finances. Know what comes in, from where (regular income, investment/ business income, bonuses, etc.) what goes out (expenses, savings, etc.) and to where. Oh, I get it, your darling husband is better at managing the household finances than you are – AWESOME – let him manage them. That being said, you should know how he does it. God forbid anything happens to him, be it death or divorce, you should not be left wondering who to pay the mortgage to, or wondering if he had life insurance or stressing about how you will manage financially, now that he and his income are gone. These are discussions to have regularly. It is unwise to hope for the best without preparing for the worst. If you haven't already had a state of the finances conversation with your spouse, after you finish this chapter make that the next thing you do. Additionally, make sure you all are having regular dialogue about your families' finances. You know how to get your husband's undivided attention – get it and keep it!

Married or not, taking action is the best way to feel — and be — in control of your money. Small steps like budgeting, cutting back on spending or boosting the amount you save each month can help. You'll feel better for taking control back — and it's good for your finances, too.

www.forbes.com/sites/forbesfinancecouncil/2017/08/08/five-reasons-women-are-taking-the-lead-in-financial-planning/#726ca36e3500

 ## Seek Help

You don't know what you don't know! It's not what you know that can hurt you but rather what you don't know. What generally causes the most pain and suffering is what you don't know that you don't know. Sometimes life will throw you curve balls that will leave you in unpredictable situations. You may not be sure what to do on your own - that's normal. If or when this happens, having coaches and advisors that you can trust, can and will make all the difference. Having support from friends and family can make it easier to manage your finances and get you unstuck. In my sessions with women, I often hear statements such as "my dad told me where to invest my money, and I haven't looked at my accounts since he died." Or I hear "I handled the bills and my husband took care of everything else." Simply put, I am embarrassed about my finances and how clueless I feel about my money. While you must seek help with your financial matters, you still need to know what's going on with them. One of my famous lines to my clients is "do your due diligence." Ask questions and make sure you understand what's happening with your money. Just like you have spiritual advisors, health and life coaches, everyone should have financial coaches as well. You should be part of the process and always be in the know about the state of your financial affairs. Seeking help is not a sign of weakness but a sign of strength.

⏻ Expectations

You might not always get what you want, but you always get what you expect! While growing up, we develop attitudes and beliefs about money. This helps shape our expectations about money - whether good or bad. While it makes sense to see the glass half full, this is not a substitute for the work that has to be put in. YOU must be willing to put your hand to the plow and WORK on your finances. Yes, you must seek help, but you must be the biggest help. Expecting the best will allow you to give the right energy to building or in some cases rebuilding your finances. If you think you can't do it or it will not work out, then you are right. If you think you can do it, you are right.

The ability to expect the best and manage financial expectations is especially critical in marriage. Money is one of the greatest stressors in many marriages. Romance without finances is nonsense. It's extremely important to talk about your financial expectations, goals, dreams, and plans. This should not be a one-time discussion, but these are topics that should be discussed on a regular basis.

Enthusiasm can go a long way. At the end of the day, without a solid financial plan and some realistic expectations, enthusiasm doesn't pay the bills.

S (Specific) What? Where? How?	
M (Measureable) From - To	
A (Assignable) Who?	
R (Realistic) Feasible?	
T (Time-based) When?	

Strength in Numbers

When an individual does something alone, there is slight strength, but where there are more than one – the strength increases. We have all heard the phrase - strength in numbers, but what does that mean? In a nutshell, it means that people with a common goal, common problem or common interest need to band together if they want to achieve change. Strength in numbers means finding others who share your fight. For example, if you are a heavy spender and that is impacting your ability to save and get your financial house in order, spend time with people who are conscientious about their spending. Join a couponing group or share your goals with others who are already good in that area and ask them to support and encourage you. Strength in numbers means we have to get past some of the hang-ups that are preventing women from becoming empowered financially. *A Women Fit Money Survey that was done in 2015 showed that 92% of women want to learn more about financial planning, yet 8 out of 10 confess they have refrained from discussing their finances with those they are close to. Only 47% of women say they would be confident discussing money and investing with a financial professional on their own. We are our Sisters Keeper and we have to learn more, so we can do more and pull each other up. We have to learn more so when our kids come to us for financial guidance we can be in position to give real and relevant information. In the words of Henry Ford: "Coming together is a beginning. Keeping together is progress. Working together is success". Ladies, we have what it takes to win financially. If you already have your financial affairs in order, find a sister friend who doesn't and teach her what you know. Make it a goal to help her hit at least one of her financial goals. When one ship rises, we all rise.

74

https://www.fidelity.com/bin-public/060_www_fidelity_com/documents/women-fit-money-study.pdf

⏻ Take Action Now

Now that you have the mental tools, below are a few basic and practical financial steps you need to take:

1.) Create a budget – A budget helps you figure out why there is always month left over at the end of the money. You must know what comes in and what goes out if you are ever going to make financial progress

2.) Protect your Income – You need 8-10 times your income in life insurance. Your greatest asset is not your home; it is your income or your ability to earn income. You need to protect it.

3.) Eliminate Debt – Reduce your use. Contrary to what you may have heard, credit cards aren't all evil. It is the misuse of them that gets many in trouble. By all means, create a strategy to pay them off, and use cash as much as you can. If most of your income is going toward debt, you will not be able to save.

4.) Pay yourself first – Put yourself at the head of the line. Treat your savings like any other recurring bill that you must pay each month.

5.) Figure out how to create your own income/business.

I know what you are saying, this is too simple. You are correct - it is. Simple enough that more women should be in better positions financially and headed towards financial freedom. It is mind over matter. The action is the easy part.

Getting past the mental setbacks is the challenge. Nothing changes if nothing changes. Once you have assessed your financial situation, YOU must take action.

Now that you have gotten through this chapter, you are responsible for what you know. Having the knowledge is not good enough, you must apply it. Were you taught Knowledge is Power? That is only partially true; Applied Knowledge is Power. Time is ticking away and like me, you are not getting any younger. If you don't start managing your finances, your legacy will suffer as a result. Leave a legacy that will empower and equip your kids to make wise financial choices As moms, what we do today will shape our kids' tomorrow. Don't let this be just another book you have read. Allow this read to not only mark a defining moment in your life but a defining moment in your legacy. The moment you decided to T.A.N. – Take Action Now!

Despite your current or past financial setbacks and challenges, know that God is a God of hope and restoration. In March of 2016. God blessed us with child # 5, Karsyn Armani. Armani means faith in African. When you marry FAITH in God with WORK - Amazing things happen!

#Live

#Laugh

#Love

#LeaveALegacy

If you would like to connect with a licensed and certified financial wellness coach and receive more answers to your financial questions, please request your complimentary copy of How Money Works, by scanning the QR code below.

Loving-Leggins & Associates

"The Architects"

Building Wealth...Building Dreams

www.primerica.com/slovingleggins

Where do you find your POWER?

I find my power in reading the Bible. I feel empowered when I'm able to empower someone else. When I tell them that they can make it with such conviction that they start to believe. I love to see the spark and the beam in their eyes when they start to believe in themselves.

Chapter 5

It's Not About How You Start

Let me begin by saying everyone has a story. I didn't realize it while I was growing up, but my story was preparing me to help other women overcome feelings of rejection, loneliness, and fear. I endured the process, so I could come alongside and help carry the next woman that needed encouragement. I am an encourager to many because I know what it feels like to want to quit because sometimes life can seem too hard. The story of my life is best summed up by saying, "it not about how you start but how you finish."

To better understand my strength, my tenacity and my will to win despite the odds, I would need to tell you about where my life began. Bear with me as I tell you the story. I hope you find yourself in some way through these pages. Although we have different backgrounds, we may have still endured the same emotional struggles. Life requires facing your truth and being able to process through your healing. We don't choose our scars. We don't choose the struggles we endure. But we do choose how we react. We have a choice to become bitter or better. I chose better.

⏻ The Beginning

I was born in Houston, Texas in the mid-1960's. I was raised during a time when African Americans were not treated or considered to be equal citizens. The struggle for African Americans during the 60's was one of great tension in society. The fight to have the same rights as other ethnicities, the right to vote, the right to the same education, and the right to be served at a restaurant was just a few of the struggles during that time for African Americans. I was born at a pivotal point in history.

I am the product of the foster care system. My young mother decided she could not care for me and placed me up for adoption at birth. Today, I am not upset with her. I have forgiven her and made my peace with her decision. On a positive note, I gained two wonderful loving parents that took care of me and showered me with love and support, since I was just three days old. Even still, I used to often wonder as a child, why she did it. I don't stand in judgment of the decision my mother made I just didn't understand why she didn't want me. As I reflect on her decision, I am thankful because she could have made a different decision and I wouldn't be here today. She carried me a healthy full-term and I will forever be grateful that she gave me life.

⏻ Rocky Start

Bringing a new life into the world should be a celebration. My birth wasn't welcomed like other babies. My first experience with the world was rejection by the one person that should have loved me. God's hands were definitely on my life from the beginning. My (adopted) mother thought it would be best to tell me at a very young age that I was adopted. She told me that even though another woman had birthed me, she wanted me. She assured me that she loved me as if she had carried me in her own stomach. She expressed that I was her daughter. She and my father made sure I knew I was loved. Finding out that I was adopted wasn't easy. It also didn't exactly create the best foundation of memories for my life. I often thought about my biological parents.

My adoptive parents met me and took me home and I never knew any other parents. Thankfully, I didn't have the horror story that we hear about children going from home to home and being abused. I wasn't abused by my parents; they took great care of me. But no matter how good they were to me, I still felt the pains of rejection from my birth mother.

My emotional issues and feelings of rejection started before I was even born. You may think that's impossible, but research has proven that babies in the womb can sense the mother's emotions. Additional research shows a fetus receives chemical signals from the mom during pregnancy that could have a negative impact on how a baby develops after birth. I believe that I felt everything my mother felt. My biological mother didn't allow herself to bond with me (her unborn child), so after I was born, I didn't connect emotionally with my adoptive family at first either. For months, and even years, I just had a place to grow but I couldn't make an emotional connection. I often thought about what my biological mother must have felt when she carried me. I wondered if she was initially excited, afraid or upset. There were just so many unanswered questions.

⏻ God Loves Me

God has always put people around me to fill it the gaps even when my parents couldn't. They did their best to provide for me; however, my father didn't make a lot of money and some of the things I wanted he wasn't always able to afford. I can remember the year that I wanted a birthday party. I wanted to be like the other little girls having birthdays, and when I turned 8 that year, I hoped for a party and pair of red, white, and blue pair of sandals I saw at a store. From previous experience, I knew there wasn't going to be a party or presents, so it was just that. I was so surprised after church one Sunday, when I walked in the fellowship hall and there were balloons, cake, and presents just for me. I opened my gift and there were the sandals I wanted. A lady in the church has purchased them. I felt so special.

My Heavenly Father showed me in more ways than one that He was orchestrating my life, and today I am so grateful for this. I hold to the scripture Jeremiah 29:11, "For I know the plans I have or you, declares the Lord, plans to prosper you and not harm you, plans to give you hope and a future." It's not how you start but how you finish.

⏻ Seed of Rejection

No matter how good things went from time to time, I couldn't help but think about her. I often wondered, what can make a mother not want her child? What was wrong with me that she didn't want to keep me? I remember when I first heard those words as an expecting mother, "you are pregnant" and I remember the excitement that began almost immediately. I started reading books, making plans for baby showers, and wondering who the baby was going to look like. I wondered if she had any of those feelings when she found out she was pregnant with me? Could a woman make the difficult decision to give her child away and experience that same excitement?

⏻ Feelings of Abandonment

Even though my adoptive parents were beautiful, growing up and well into my adult life, I still dealt with issues of abandonment and rejection. In my young mind, I often imagined my frightened mother sitting with a caseworker in a cold room. I imagined the caseworker advising her of her rights, telling her that they can only provide her unborn child with basics needs, shelter and food and how once she signs the dotted line she will relinquish her rights as my mother. That messed me up emotionally as a child because I couldn't understand why she didn't need me like I needed her.

I started noticing signs of rejection creeping up in different areas of my life as I grew older. I never formed long-lasting relationships. There was always this thought in the back of my mind that I was going to be abandoned. I didn't trust people to stay with me long and now that I look back over things I would leave a friendship or relationship at the first sign of trouble; before they could leave me.

I found myself being very clingy to my parents I never wanted to go anywhere without them. As I look back on it, I'm sure I was a little annoying to them not ever having time away from me. I remember a few instances my mother wasn't home when I got home from school and I automatically thought the worse. I always thought something had happened or she wasn't coming back. What an intense state for a child to live in.

Feelings of Rejection shows up in different forms. Overcoming these issues was very difficult for me because I didn't know what I was dealing with. I didn't know how to label it. What I did know, was that it was hard for me to develop long-lasting relationships with other people. Of course, I realize not every person you meet is supposed to be in a deep relationship with you, however emotionally I knew something was wrong with me. I often felt I needed to protect myself in a relationship. Self-preservation kept showing its head. I thought I had to protect myself, my feelings, and emotions, after all, no one else was going to do it. I had a tough outer core as a front but in actuality, I was so vulnerable. I felt alone.

⏻ The Power of Forgiveness

I finally had the chance to meet my birth mother at the age of 25. I felt this was necessary to do, as I wanted to get closure to that chapter in my life. The first thing she asked when she saw me was, "Are you mad at me?" I wasn't mad at her. I had forgiven her and released the hurt I felt from what she did. I responded, "no I'm not mad I've had a great life." She said, "I'm glad because I didn't want to give you up but I had to; I couldn't take care of you." She went on to say how she loved me and told me that she looked in at me, at the hospital nursery when I was born. She told me I was a beautiful little girl. I felt such a strong love for this woman, although we had just met for a few hours. I loved her, and it didn't matter anymore why she decided to give me up.

I quickly saw that she still wasn't capable of being a mother to me. Frankly, I don't know what I wanted or expected from her. She was very sickly and needed someone to care for her. I pondered with myself, do I take on this responsibility of taking care of this woman who gave me away without much thought? I decided to take her in and do what I could for her. She stayed with my family and me and I cared for her until she was ready to go back home in Houston. We didn't ever quite establish a mother-daughter relationship, but I learned to love and respect her.

Three years later I met my biological father. Although he accepted me as his daughter at his request, we kept it a secret about me, because he was concerned about his reputation. I was alright with that, after all, I had siblings and I was able to bond with them. I am glad for the time I had with my biological parents. I was able to have some questions answered and gain more family.

My adopted mother passed away in 1990 just a few months after meeting my birth mother. That was the loneliest time in my life. One morning during my devotional time God gave me the scripture Psalms 27:10, it says, "Even if my father and mother abandon me, the Lord will hold me close." After God gave me this scripture every time I would feel the spirit of loneliness or rejection coming upon me I would read the scripture and I feel better.

⏻ Abandoned Dreams

I knew from the age of 5 that I wanted to be a teacher. My mother was my preschool teacher and everything she taught us during the day school I would make the kids sit down at recess, and I would teach it again. I had my life planned to go to college and become a teacher. Somewhere along the way, I abandoned my dream. We often look at abandonment as someone leaving you or rejecting you, but sometimes we abandon ourselves. I felt hopeless, I had given up on me, but I now know that God never gave up on me.

⏻ Dream Again

My parents were set on me getting married and having children. So, I married and had children two boys and two girls (one of my girls is my heavenly baby). I wanted a marriage like my parents had. I had what everyone else considered to be the dream life; the husband, children, dog, and the white picket fence. But even with all of that, I was unhappy because I had lost myself. I had buried my dream. I suffered in silence because I didn't want to appear to be ungrateful for what I had and the life we had made. I was unhappy, sad, and unfilled in the relationship. I felt like my husband didn't understand me nor did he care about how I felt as long as his needs were met. So, I did what any "good woman" was supposed to do. I took care of my family and lived my life vicariously through my children.

Everything I did was about my children. I made sure they knew I loved them and was their biggest supporter. Still, I wanted more out of life... I wanted a career. I felt like I had no outlet, no one to talk to that would understand. I suffered from emotional abuse even physical abuse at times. My only outlet was to leave but I cared about what people thought about my husband and me, after all, he was a preacher. I had lost myself.

I Had to Find Me

Divorce isn't an overnight decision, it's something that I contemplated for years, but it was a decision I knew I had to make. I stuck with the marriage as long as I did for my sons. I felt they needed their father. When I left my husband, it was the biggest, boldest and scariest move I had ever made. This was the first time I lived on my own and supported myself financially. I knew that it would take a miracle to sustain me and my daughter. How was I going to make it? I thought over and over again to myself.

Our divorce became a legal battle. I was being dragged in and out of court every other week; I was so exhausted. I was ready to give up. I drove up to my house one day and when I put my foot out of the door, there was a leaflet from the bible laying there. I picked it up and read it; it was Psalms 68. "Let God arise, let his enemies be scattered." That's all I read and I begin to cry I knew without a shadow of doubt God had my back on that situation. The very next time I had to go to court, the judge threw the frivolous case out. I knew I was going to win this battle with God on my side. He already knew the plans he had for me from the beginning.

⏻ Big Goals…Big Steps

I enrolled in college and I worked hard to rediscover the dream I had abandoned. I finished with the first degree and I went for the second one. I was so excited my hard work was paying off I was getting ready to walk across the stage with my Bachelor's in Education. When the Chancellor called my name all I could hear was my children applauding and screaming for me. That was one of the proudest moments for me. My children were my biggest cheerleaders… the tables had turned.

⏻ I Did It

There were times I felt overwhelmed, tired, stressed, and wanted to give up but I knew I couldn't. I would call a friend and ask that she would pray with me and she would stop right then and pray. I worked a full-time and a part-time job and registered for two classes a semester. I was very strategic in how I scheduled work and school, so I could still be available for my children. I learned to trust God in this journey. My parents gave me the foundation of prayer and I prayed and prayed for God to lead and guide me through this process.

When I thought I was alone, God would always remind me of Jeremiah 29:11.

This hasn't been an easy journey, but it has made me the person I am today. My children and I went through some hard times, but we remained committed to what we wanted to be in life. I can proudly say that I was a good example, all of my children have attended college and have successful careers and businesses.

Although it hasn't been easy, I want you to know that you can make it no matter what your circumstances are. God is faithful to His word and will see you through if you just trust Him. When I look back and wonder how I made it, I think about the famous poem, Footprints in the Sand. I realize God was carrying me. And no matter what you are going through God will carry you.

I learned some things about myself that I hope will help you on your journey of life. We all deal with hurt and abandonment, but we don't have to become a victim to it.

The first thing I had to do was stop pretending I was stronger than I was. To everyone, I was this strong, tough woman. I thought I had to prove to the world that I was so strong and could withstand anything. That was the furthest thing from the truth.

Secondly, I had to begin to accept the real person I was and *acknowledge that* I needed an overhaul. I was a woman with some weakness and strengths. It wasn't until after my divorce I begin to work on me. I wanted to be a better person all around, better mother and friend.

Thirdly, I stopped comparing myself to other women; I had my own journey. It seemed like everybody else had it all together but me. I was amazed at the progress I made when I started concentrating on me. It opened up so many other avenues for me.

Fourthly, I learned to celebrate me and not feel guilty about it. For some reason, I didn't know how to celebrate me. If I wanted to go to a movie, I didn't wait for someone to ask me out, I went to the movie by myself. If I wanted a meal from a certain place, I would go by myself. That was a huge accomplishment for me because there was a time I didn't know how to celebrate me.

Lastly, when those feelings started to creep up again because they will, I reminded myself of who I am. I am the daughter of the King. I am the head and not the tail. I am an overcomer, and everything that concerns me concerns the Heavenly Father.

In life, you will either give up or go for what you want. My road hasn't always been easy, but because my will to win was stronger, I found a way. By the grace of God, I discovered who I was meant to be. Most people could not have endured, survived, or created the life that God has allowed for me to have. I am thankful to have not only experience this life with my children but now with my grandchildren. It's not about how you start, but how you finish.

I have my children whom I love with every core of my being; I was determined that they would always know I loved them and I would always be there for them. I'm blessed to have seven little people that I am Mimi to, and I love them very much. I am in my happy place. My children and I are survivors, and we hold each other up.

Remember it's not how you start but how you finish. God knows the plans He has for you, you have to trust the process.

Meet: Dr. Kanini Brooks

Where do you find your POWER?

Prayer, praise and trust in a loving, grace-giving, mighty and trustworthy God. God has the final say I and He walks, talks, provides, encourages, empowers, emboldens and orchestrates for me all things for my good. He is continuously growing and preparing me for my NEXT.

Chapter 6

Growing Pains
(The Process of Finding Purpose)

I am a Seed Planter, Encourager, and a Connector. I wish I could say I have always known that. In fact, it has only been in the last seven years or so that I have been able to put that phrase together concerning my purpose. One thing I can say, however, is there were certain things I knew about myself early on, would somehow be part of the future me. It took a process of growth to recognize, own and embrace the twists and turns in my life. Those things are the growing pains that have brought me to this point.

I would imagine if you took some time to look back over your own life, you would find that on the other end of your hardest, darkest, most challenging seasons of life - when you were stretched the most - you actually matured and learned the most about yourself. These times served as unique opportunities to see what you were made of and how far you could go. I like to think of these pivotal times in our life as 'growth spurts.'

⏻ **Growing Pains**

Of course, you have heard the phrase "growing pains" at some point in life. "Growing pains" refers to the literal pains many young people experience in their limbs as they grow in stature. As their arms and legs lengthen and the bones and joints extend to stretch their body, the actual hurt is reported, especially at night. For those of us not familiar with this original sense of the phrase, we have heard "growing pains" used in reference to struggles, sufferings and various difficult situations we find ourselves in along the journey of life. When this phrase is invoked, it is as if to say, "these struggles are part of the process of growing up and becoming an adult."

Growing pains are designed to lengthen or stretch you. Growth is a process that we all must endure – and not just physically but mentally and spiritually. Although we would love to arrive at point A to point Z without any inconveniences, pain or discomfort, that is not the way we were created. One thing I have learned about God is that everything He does has a divine order. Everything that He has made goes through a process of growth. Whether it is a person or a tree, nothing comes out fully grown or fully matured.

⏻ **The Growth Process (Stages)**

Let's consider a seed and how it grows continually over time. The seed evolves through various stages and processes of growth ultimately taking its place in nature as a fully-grown tree. Think about some of the stages a tree endures as compared to our human process of growth.

The first stage is the discovery process for the seed. For example, a tree is not born a tree. It begins as a tiny seed. After the initial process, the seed gets 'buried' under the dirt – as if it were dead - before life can be seen. Now, consider your life. You know that you were created for a purpose; your purpose is your "seed." Just like the tree, your seed is buried on the inside of you waiting to be uncovered.

Next, that buried seed must grab hold of its foundation by growing roots underground. For you, this underground process is where you receive all of your tools necessary for growth. Your underground foundation is the cultivation of your morals, your character traits, your position and value in this world. More than likely, these roots were formed in a family environment. Upon establishing its roots, the tiny seed must find the strength to burst through the dirt and sprout forth a leaf. It is still not yet a tree. Over time, the roots strengthen, and a sprout reaches further as it continues to grow additional leaves and forms a trunk. Year after year, slow to the eye, continuous growth is taking place. Do you remember when you made your first steps sprouting out of the place where you received your foundation? The first day of school is a great example of this. In this new environment, you thrived as you started to grow. It was there you learned how to make new friends and what it felt like to break out of your familiar comfort zone. You encountered many things socially that contributed to your growth. You gained friends, and you lost friends, but you grew stronger. Just like the tree.

As we grow as humans, our growth pattern follows a similar course. We overcome obstacles and challenges nearly every day. Depending on how strong our roots are, we can weather the storms and come back stronger, bigger and better. Or, if we aren't strong enough, we may bend, break or worse-wither up and die, like the leaves on a tree.

⏻ The Pruning Process

The pruning stage is a painful process. For the benefit of the rest of the journey, the key is to recognize this stage, grieve any loss you may experience and recover from it. No matter what you encounter, you must rebound from this stage. Don't stay in it. Instead, identify the lessons learned to carry with you through the rest of your life's journey. A tree that is pruned is only pruned to get rid of the dead leaves and anything else preventing it from growing and coming into its own. And so, it is with us, painful as it may seem at the time, growth comes with a price. The pruning process is also necessary for the growth of the tree, and just like a tree, we must withstand our painful yet essential process. Our pruning process includes life's storms and difficulties. When we lose or experience a significant change in any area, the aftermath or results from this progression manifests itself in our psyche or our emotions. As we grow, we must constantly evaluate whether the pruning process has changed the way we see ourselves or how we see others. If we are not careful we can become angry and bitter, assuming the pruning is a negative thing instead of a positive life course.

Self-Reflection

It is good for us to periodically take an inventory of our lives and reflect on how far we've come. Always take the time to take inventory and remember the dreams. Think about where you want your life to be and get inspired to pursue them. Dreams keep us alive and push us to pursue our purpose. "Without a vision the people perish" (Proverbs 29:18). Dreams literally give us life.

Dreams are Seeds

Your dreams are seeds. In many cases, those big dreams about who we wanted to be when we grew up, what kind of life we wanted to live in our adult life, whom we would marry and what family life would be like, began with a mere thought – a seed. As we meditated on those feelings, they grew - transforming those seeds into thoughts. When we began to verbalize the thought, perhaps with friends or family, it grew roots. The thought grew legs (leaves) that turned into action steps. Without even realizing it, we gathered information, prepared ourselves – possibly unwittingly, maybe even on 'auto-pilot.' Did you know that your conversation can induce manifestation? Not convinced? Consider right now what you spent the most time talking about earlier in your life. Sit and reflect on how some of those ideas and goals eventually manifested in your life. You may not see manifestation in every area, just yet, but keep living and you will see how it unfolds for you. Be careful what you say with your mouth, your body will follow and very likely will come to pass.

What does this look like in real life? I can tell you how it worked out for me. I ALWAYS knew I was a teacher. But, I would say, "I'm a teacher but just not in the traditional way." I knew I was not supposed to be a regular classroom teacher. It was my goal as a high school student to become an engineer and make lots of money and have my money working for me, so I could teach and not have to worry about the money. In the past few years, I have realized that I am more of an 'educator' than a teacher. To me, the word educator encompasses so much more than teaching. Teaching is more finite concerning training someone in a particular skill or giving him or her some information or knowledge. Educating involves developing and empowering someone, more like a coach. Once I discovered the difference, things I was experiencing in my life started to make sense.

⏻ Walking in Purpose

I was thrust into my purpose through a series of divine interventions, including receiving my engineering degree and moving across the country for my first Engineering job. After only eleven short months of working, I was laid off from my new job. I didn't anticipate that (pruning) would happen that way. I found myself looking for employment. I ran across a job in the newspaper; the ad was for a mathematics specialist. It turned out that it was a job teaching high-level math to elementary school children using the Socratic method. I knew that would be a great fit for me given my educational background. And although I did not go to school and earn a teaching certificate, I landed the job and ended up teaching in a non-traditional way – like I always said I wanted to. Not only did I teach elementary school children, but I taught junior high, high school, conducted professional development workshops for teachers and ultimately became the community and family involvement liaison on the leadership team. It would be many years before I made the connections between this season of preparation and my purpose. I have been developing my "teaching" ever since, evolving into the Educator I am today.

When I reflect on what I have learned about life, I know that not all change is bad. All of my circumstances, surroundings, the circle of associates and my friends shaped me, fed me, and groomed (or prepared) me for my purpose. I did not plan it that way. But the 'teachers' in my life showed up – sometimes at the hardest points in my life to help guide me to my purpose. I also learned a lot about myself in the process. I have found that I am more resilient than I thought. I also recognized I could take risks and come out on top. Most importantly, I know for a fact that everything that happens in my life all works out for my good. My job is to trust the process. After all, it is all part of the growth process.

These days, I do not have to go through anything traumatic to identify how I have grown. I simply take the time to look at myself and ask the question: What am I doing right now, that I was not or could not have been able to do even a year ago? How did I learn that lesson? Every obstacle, unexpected setback, challenge, etc. has ended up working out in my favor. Even when it seemed impossible and particularly inconvenient, it all worked out!

⏻ Follow the Breadcrumbs

The good news is, God does not just orchestrate things divinely only for me. He does it for each of us. Have you heard of the boy scout exercise with breadcrumbs the scouts participate in when they go camping? It is simple and makes sense. When they go out into the woods, they leave little breadcrumbs along their path so if they get lost, they can find the path of breadcrumbs and find their way back. For us, God does that in reverse. God has left breadcrumbs in the 'forest' of this world despite all the noise and all the distractions, twists and turns on life's journey – both joys and sorrows - that lead you right to Him and to the purpose He placed in you. As we become more mature in our ability to recognize those breadcrumbs, the easier it will become to feel His 'nudge' into the direction He would have us to go. You'll be able to see His hand moving all around you. Recognition of this process is ultimate growth.

⏻ Trust the Process

I heard someone say that if we knew what lay ahead on the journey, we might not go at all. Most of the time we may only see one step at a time. Or maybe we can only see a short stretch of the road at a time. God never shows us the entire path. Trusting the process is the easiest thing to do if we learn to just surrender to it. When we encounter the unknown or the uncomfortable the human reaction is to hesitate or give up. If we could just get our minds wrapped around the fact that we cannot experience the glory of our purpose or our future without the process, it might be an

100

easier pill to swallow. Again, we do not come into this earth trusting the process. We grow into that mindset. We develop a thirst and a hunger for the things that are aligned with who we were created to be.

 ## Power of Reflection

The power of reflection is key. When you look back and see how you have grown and been kept, prepared, and strengthened, you can rest in knowing you are in good hands. The sooner we learn this, the better we are. I am glad I know it now. It took me leaving my comfort zone to finally get there. It took me getting into places where there was no one else to run to, in order to finally get here.

 ## When Purpose Finds You

It's funny how when you have aligned with purpose even the most unlikely situations work out in your favor. I found myself meeting the man I would marry during one of the most inconvenient times of my life. I had recently endured a huge change in my travel schedule at work, which forced me to travel over 40+ plus miles every day back and forth. I also answered the call for "help" to serve in the youth choir at the church I was attending. Both work and church were clear on the opposite side of town, and it made my commute excruciating. Everything seemed wrong about the situation. When I received the initial invitation from the church I wanted to decline. But God nudged and orchestrated the circumstances in such a way that I did not have time to think, analyze or come up with the excuses not to accept the invitation. What had I gotten myself into I thought?

After taking on the new responsibility, things didn't seem to be working out too well for me. I threatened to leave the church a few times, but I stayed because God rearranged everything to ensure I was in the right place. After about nine months of serving, I met my husband. Some may call it a coincidence, but I know it was because I was aligned with purpose. I met him on the same exact day an offer I had put in for a home was accepted by the homeowner, which placed me closer to the area. I ended up staying at the church a little over 2 years. I later left to join my new husband at his church which was less than a mile from the church I was originally called to. Fully prepared and equipped for my NEXT level.

The lesson I learned was that when you are doing what He wants you to do, He is with you, He equips you, and He sends you what you need to endure when it gets hard. He grows you and He rewards you. Bottom line: I had to be pushed out of my comfort zone to grow into a position for my future husband to find me. I had to endure discomfort long enough for that to happen. I learned to trust God and the truth in the Bible verse "[His] thoughts are not [our] thoughts, neither are [our] ways [His] ways" (Isaiah 55:9). *

⏻ He's Right on Time

I cannot emphasize enough how important it is to remember to look back to see His hand orchestrating, instructing, guiding, helping, equipping, providing, loving, blessing, keeping, using and growing you. What I learned during those two years at that church has sustained me as I continue to serve in ministry, and work in the community.

He knows what He is doing. We just have to press. He is always right on time and has our best interest in mind. "For He knows the plans He has for us (Jeremiah 29:11)."

Growing in Grace is a Choice

Don't miss out on your blessing trying to avoid discomfort and inconvenience. Let's talk about what happens when you do not grow in grace. Some negative alternatives to the growth process are bitterness, anger, self-pity, placing blame and adding to the list of excuses for being 'stuck.' When you face challenges do you choose to stay stuck, mad at the world, or do you willingly accept your current situation as the "new normal"? Life can be a series of lessons to be learned. Some will bring us joy. Some will bring us grief. Others will leave us confused, while still others will try us to see what we are made of. Each season's lesson is different. However, what they all have in common is 'they all pass." The seasons or events do not last forever. Just like the tree experiences seasons of growth, flourishing, pruning, and even some parts dying off, so do we. The good news is, if we take the time to reflect on these seasons, we will discover that combined, each contributed in some way to who we are as a person – good, bad or ugly.

Every time you "learned a lesson," changed your perspective or gained more confidence or wisdom on something or someone you were dealing with, it came at a price. The price of extending, growing and taking you to higher heights. Don't let that cost of that "stretch," be in vain. Consider: Did I go through all of this for someone else?

⏻ It's Bigger than You

I do not believe our growth process is only for ourselves. Our growing pains ought to be beneficial to others. They ought to help others avoid some mistakes we have made or make some lessons be learned easier than the hard way we learned them.

Oh, how we think we are doing things on our own. Little do we know when we are just "living life," that He is intentional about what He allows in your life. He knows exactly what you need and how far you will go with whom. He knows what experiences, circumstances, and relationships it will take to shape and grow you into who you are to be for the next season. He does it, again and again, moving you into your purpose. No season in your life that you find yourself in is a surprise to Him. He is always working on your behalf – and mine. Sometimes it's painful. It's just growing pains. That's Him stretching you, preparing you for what you are not ready for right now. Are you willing to accept that He knows what He is doing and that it is time to trust the growth process?

If you are ready to endure the growth process takes some time to ask yourself: "What events or seasons in my life influenced me to be the stronger, wiser, better woman I am today?

List at least three of them that come to mind quickly below.

1)

2)

3)

⏻   Reflection

Now that you've read my story and my growing pains let's bring it home. Ask yourself some reflection questions as you think about the pains you have endured. Take some time to think about the good and bad situations that have contributed to your growth process.

What did you learn about yourself (e.g., confidence; self-love; strength; wisdom; desires; dreams; or something else)?

How did you encourage yourself and/or find the strength to press through difficult times?

What have you learned about people, life and God as a result?

Would you take the experience(s) back if you could? Why or why not?

Think about where you made mistakes, what it cost you, what you learned (about yourself, about life, and about others). What would you have done differently, if anything?

How can you help your children through their "growth spurts," should these learnings show up in your parenting?

To avoid your children from having to go through the same things you had to go through or make the same mistake(s) you made, what do you need to teach your children?

As you consider these events and situations, think about how the result of those growth stages show up in how you live your life today. Remember, if He entrusted you with the journey, you can trust your children with the story (age appropriate sharing of details, of course). After all, He entrusted you with the children He gave you. The more I reflected on my life at different points in my life; I found that various relationships had shaped, groomed, fed and prepared me for other ones.

We earn our stripes every day. We learn what to do and what not to do. Sometimes we fall and get a little scraped up but, hopefully, we stop to look into the mirror and remember to make decisions that help lead us to our purpose.

Meet Trina Smith

Where do you find your POWER?

I find my power when I am reading my bible, the more I read the word, the more I find myself being strengthened, renewed and empowered.

Chapter 7

Beautifully Restored

I'm the mother of eight beautiful children, and before your mind begins to race let me answer all of your typical questions. Yes... I have cable. Yes... I have a good paying job. Yes... I have a life. And yes... I am happily married. I've probably spent half of my adult life defending myself, my choices, and my children until one day I realized I didn't owe anyone an explanation for my life. I also realized not only had God made me special enough to be able to give birth to eight healthy babies, but I was also fearfully made in His image, and my story was unique. I've experienced the harsh judgment of others, which although their lives weren't storybook perfect, they saw fit to judge me based on the choices I had made for my life.

According to statistics, I should not be successful today, but God had a different plan for me. He knew He could entrust me with this journey. I am indeed blessed! Despite all of the shameful things I went through; the looks, the ridicule, the insensitive jokes and negative comments... I survived! It wasn't easy, but my life was beautifully restored.

My life headline once read: "Two months old baby girl, abandoned by her mother and given to a friend of the family to be raised." Some called her mother, Aunt Willie, Mother Mathis-Fanniel and Big Mama. I called her mom because she was the only mother I ever knew; until the day I was introduced to my biological mother. I didn't quite understand the dynamics of what was going on; I felt like I was frozen for a moment in time. I was in shock. Anyone in my situation would feel neglected, abandoned and not wanted by their biological mother, but that was not my story. My God-given mom taught me to forgive, love and care for others. Finding out I had "another" mother didn't change much for me. I was happy to meet her and wanted to get to know her, and I did. But even after the introduction, I continued to stay with my mom. She cared for me as if she was my birth mom, doing the things that mothers do.

I was raised in the church, so you can imagine how my life was turned upside down when I became pregnant at the age of 17 years old. It was totally unexpected, and I can admit that I was not prepared to be a mother. I was a scared teenager, pregnant out of wedlock and still in high school. I kept looking at myself saying, "I have messed up big time." I remember having all of these terrifying thoughts about my life; they constantly ran through my mind. I literally felt every negative thing people said about being young and pregnant. I was frantic... What am I going to do?... How can I afford to take care of a baby, when I'm a baby myself?... How could I be so stupid to allow this to happen to me "the church girl"?...

How can I get rid of the baby without anyone ever knowing? I had all of these thoughts and much more running through my head. I didn't know how I would face my grandmother, my mom, my boyfriend or my church. I wanted to crawl under a rock and die. Little did I know, that facing them would be only half the battle. In that moment of my life, I learned that every decision I made, I had to consider everyone that would be affected, hurt and involved in my process. Whether it was a good, bad or ugly choice, I had to consider all involved!

I finally confessed to my mom about the pregnancy, she was disappointed in me and hurt all at the same time. Although she was upset with me, she showed me that she still loved me. "You have to get married because it is the right thing to do," was what she told me. I had never planned to get married at such a young age. I felt pressured. I felt so alone. I wasn't ready to get married. What was I to do? I felt hopeless; she wasn't giving me a choice. I was nervous about my future. I was still just a child myself. But, I wanted to do the right thing by my unborn child and my mom. Throughout the entire pregnancy, I wondered if I would be good enough for this child. I had many doubts. I didn't think I was ready… I didn't think we were ready.

When the father and I agreed to keep our child, I was told we would have to stand up before the church and ask for forgiveness. Now to add more salt to a wound that was already hurting, I had to build up the nerves to stand before those hypocritical folks and shine a light on what I had done. I agreed to go in front of the church and to do what was required of me.

I remember that day as if I was standing there today. All eyes were on me, waiting with anticipation of what would come out of my mouth as I walked down the aisle and headed towards the pulpit area. After service I was asked by some of the members "how did this happen"? "Well, umm"... The condescending eyes of judgment looked at me, making me feel guiltier and more ashamed. I could not wait to walk out of those church doors and go home, just so I could not be asked any more questions, and be looked at as if I were wearing some scarlet letter. I am sure I wasn't the only one having sex without being married in the church. I was just one of the ones that got caught. I am thankful that my godparents stayed with me throughout the ordeal; they encouraged me and let me know I wasn't alone.

 Baby #1

I really bonded with my baby during my pregnancy. I remember feeling my baby move for the first time and I thought something was wrong, I was tickled to discover this was a normal part of the pregnancy. I used to lay on the sofa and watch my baby move up and down in my stomach, what an amazing feeling it was - it looked like something from a scary movie. It was in those moments all the negative looks and crossed stares didn't matter anymore, I was in love with these moments my baby and I would share. I became stronger, and I didn't let the negativity from anyone bother me much anymore. I cherished those moments at home in my safe place.

As a senior in high school, I was placed in an alternative school for pregnant teens. It was kind of an embarrassment at times for me, being placed in a school like that. I knew better than to get pregnant, at least that's what I thought. Before I got pregnant, my Mother would always say "don't you have sex, because you will get pregnant and if you get pregnant you're not going to live here with a baby." Now looking back, I wished I could have gotten more information on why it's important to be a virgin and keep yourself for the husband God has for you. I wish I would have known about the spiritual ties that sexual intercourse creates. But I'm sure my mom told me the best way she knew how. She was in her 60's, raising a teenager girl and I'm sure that had to be tough on her as well.

⏻   **Eighteen**

I was eighteen, a new mother and married. Was this really my life? I wondered. I was still trying to make sense of how things were going to turn out for me. I wasn't emotionally, financially or physically prepared for this life; however, the world didn't stop or slow down for me to try and figure it out. I wondered if God would forgive me for having a baby or what others considered "my mistake?" I'm glad He is a God of second chances. Because of knowing that, I was able to survive the pregnancy, my new life, and all that came with it.

It was finally time to give birth; it was a Friday morning at 6 AM. I remembered it was a Friday because it was also Homecoming at our school. My family came to the hospital to support me; my sisters, cousins and even my mom came to sit with me and keep me calm and relaxed. Labor was intense; I had never felt pain like I did that day. They tried everything to comfort me, but no ice chips or back rubs was enough to soothe the pain. All I could do was pray, breathe, pray and breathe some more. It didn't minimize the pain, but it did relax me. I didn't have an epidural or any medicine, I toughed it out and kept doing what relaxed me the most. I remembered the nurses talking to me about pushing. Right in the middle of labor, I got scared and panicked. I told myself I'm not going to be able to do this. It was true. I had worked up my nerves and my fears, and right in the middle of giving birth, I stopped pushing. The nurses had to talk me through the process step by step, and after the last push, I was a mother for the first time.

Surprise

After having my son, I wanted to lose the little weight I'd gained during the pregnancy. My husband and I at the time decided to get a membership at a gym. After only a few months, I remember feeling a little sick and having to vomit while working out. I didn't know what was wrong, so I made an appointment to see my doctor, I was surprised that it was not the flu or a common cold — I was pregnant again... and just like that, Baby #2 was on the way. I had just given birth less than a few months ago, and I was already pregnant with another one. What in the world was going on with me? Life was moving very quickly.

⏻ The Baby's Here

One early morning while sitting at my grandmother in law's house I went into labor. I was trying to stay calm and breathe, but the contractions got so heavy that I knew it was time to give birth. I arrived at the hospital, went upstairs to the labor and delivery room, and before I knew it the baby was ready to come out. I wasn't in the labor room for long before I was the mother of a beautiful baby girl and a 19-month-old baby boy. I felt excited and overwhelmed at the same time. I brought my baby girl home from the hospital, the day before Mother's Day. I was ready to love her and protect her. I remember one special moment I had with my daughter after bringing her home from the hospital. I was sitting on the sofa holding her and I looked down at her with love in my eyes, and I heard myself say the words "how can a mother give her daughter away?" I realized then that I had never dealt with the feelings of hurt from my mother giving me away. I had internalized and buried the feelings, but I needed to be healed from them. It was probably the first time I felt abandoned, rejected and neglected all at the same time. I had never processed my emotions before, but at that moment I decided to love my mother regardless of how I felt about how she'd abandoned me.

⏻ Positive Results

My entire world became taking care of my two babies. There wasn't a waking moment that you didn't see me with both of them. Every time we left the house, whether it was going to the store or church, I would have to prepare a diaper bags and bottles and everything they needed. I carried one child in a car seat while holding the other's one hand. It was like doing a juggling act at times, but I enjoyed doing it. And after my baby girl was only a few months old, I started to feel a little sick. So, I did what had I done before; I bought another pregnancy test... just to check. I couldn't believe that I was sitting in the bathroom taking another pregnancy test waiting on the results... shaking and scared at the same time. How could this be happening? I thought I was on birth control. All types of questions flashed before my head as I sat waiting for the results. No matter how hard I wished for different results, the results would be positive (+). I sat in the bathroom wanting to scream. I remember hiding the pregnancy for some months because I didn't want to hear any negative talk from anyone, but it was only a few months until I started showing. In the back of my mind, I thought I could hide the whole thing and never have to speak about it. I know that sounds crazy, but when you're pregnant with now the third child, you forget what God said about "be fruitful and multiply." You become more consumed with what people say, instead of what He says. I have to say it was God who helped me to get through these moments in my life; I truly had to rely on Him. Before I knew it, I was in the delivery room with baby #3.

 Reality Sets In

Taking caring of three babies was exhausting. There were times my mind would shut down and I would open my mouth for help, but no one could hear me. I felt like I had no control over my emotions. I was often left home alone with three children all under the age of 3, it was difficult to say the least. I remember seeing myself in a daze on one particular day holding my crying baby, and walking right out of front door of the apartment leaving them there by themselves just so I could get some quiet. I was secretly battling with some deep dark emotions. I was later able to put a name to what I was feeling. Postpartum. It was something I had heard briefly about but I had no idea that it was a REAL disease. I didn't know what was happening to me. I knew I loved my kids, and there was no denying that, but there was something going on with me emotionally and I couldn't explain it. Postpartum depression is a very dark place and I found myself visiting that place frequently, fighting those emotions and telling myself "come on Trina, snap out of it." I didn't realize the depth of it. I didn't know that I was in the middle of the battle for my mind and emotions, fighting sometimes on a daily basis. I remember being so exhausted and sleep deprived, feeling as if I had no control over my emotions until one day I decided to talk to my doctor about the way I was feeling. My doctor took the time to explain to me what was happening and for the first time I heard an in-depth explanation of this sickness. After her dialogue with me, she decided to put me on Prozac. I didn't want to take it because I didn't want to rely on medicine to give me a sense of balance. I chose not to take the medication and of course I did not tell her my decision either. What I did choose was what I heard my mother do when she needed help. I got on my knees and began talking to my Father God about these crazy emotions that were going on inside and I desperately

116

asked Him to remove them. I'm not sure how long it took, but I do remember those emotions suddenly began to dwindle away and I felt a sense of myself again. I no longer wanted to harm myself or my children. It was then I realized it was God who allowed me to survive that dark place. I rose out of that depressive state of mind. I was finally free of that disease they called postpartum depression. It's a real thing and I encourage all moms to be honest with themselves and talk about it with their doctors; along with their spouses.

Sickness... Again

I caught the flu and was so sick and weak that I could barely get out of bed. I called the doctor and went in for a checkup. The doctor confirmed I had the flu and I was pregnant. What in the world was going on? I remember sitting in the doctor's office saying how is that possible? I was on birth control, but apparently, it was NOT strong enough. I looked at the doctor in amazement — this was crazy. I was doing everything I knew to prevent the pregnancies but I still ended up getting pregnant. It seemed like my own body was against me. I sat in the doctor's office and I cried, I felt so ashamed. She had just delivered my third baby, earlier this year and now, I was pregnant with my fourth child. All I could think was "here we go again." I could never get over the stares and the negative things people would say. I did not want to be pregnant! I wanted to crawl under a rock and never return, if possible.

I couldn't go to church, store, park or any place without somebody asking, "Are all of those kids yours?" I tried to be polite and offer up a smile, but in my mind I was saying "here we go again." I'd seen people be happy that they were having a baby, however, I couldn't have those feelings because I was too busy worrying and giving other people power with their words. I would go on to try and hide the pregnancy from everyone as long as I could until my clothes started getting too tight for me. We do things to ourselves to hide and satisfy the needs of others all because we think we can't handle the pressure of what one may say about us. I fell into this trap, year after year. I sometimes allowed what others said about my pregnancies to make me not want to be pregnant or have joy.

Brokenness

Crying was a common thing for me during my pregnancy. I would sit inside the shower sometimes and cry, so no one could hear the brokenness I carried inside. I put on the mask daily, when I dealt with others, just to survive the words people might say to me, whether it was intentional or unintentional. I was pregnant with baby #4. Months would pass, the baby was moving and I would still be excited about these moments when I was in the comfort of my home. I had given the power to people whose words didn't count towards my life. Some people would ask me, are you a baby making machine? I would laugh like it was funny, all the while I felt like a bug squashed under a rock. Besides just being pregnant, I felt like I needed to do something different. I joined a CNA program and became licensed by the state, I was so excited about the journey. I would go to class every day and I would get home in time to have dinner cooked, family fed, kids bathed and ready for bed. That was my nightly routine. I enjoyed it. It was my life; my family was my everything.

A Big Decision

After my fifth pregnancy, I decided to get the Depo-Provera shot to prevent myself from going through this again. The shot worked for 2 ½ years, but boy did I suffer for it. It messed with my attitude and I was not myself. While changing my birth control at that time, I learned that I was pregnant with my sixth child. This time I had enough. I decided I wasn't going to keep the baby. I made an appointment and went in to have an abortion. I refused to be subjected to the negative energy of others for another pregnancy. Abortion would be my answer and I would fix everybody else, so I thought. As I sat at the abortion clinic sitting in the waiting area with my husband, I was so afraid. I had no idea what was going to happen; I sat there wondering would it hurt?... Would they put me to sleep? I had so many questions. I couldn't go through with it. I walked out of the abortion clinic. My beautiful chunky baby was born later that year, and I could not thank God enough.

Restoration

I am amazed at where my life started and how it evolved to where it is today. I can truly say that God has been good to my family and me. I married the love of my life and we now have a blended family of 11 kids. Our children remind us why God put us on this earth; to be fruitful and multiply.

Being a mother is not easy, but it is rewarding. When God chose to plant a seed in your womb, He counted your worth. Children are a gift from God, no matter what others may say. I was once the young lady that thought I would graduate from high school and go off to nursing school to become a nurse. My life went down a different path, but I am glad to say that God knew what was best. I overcame a lot of struggles, and I made it out on top.

Deep down inside I knew I could make it through if I would submit everything to God... I remember during one of my last pregnancies, I was driving in my car, crying and wondering if I would make it through this because sometimes the painful words of others would be greater than what God said. I started to pray and ask God to remove this pain from me and help me not to let other people's words take ownership of me. I cried out, "God I want to be free from people and walk in the peace and freedom found in you, help me Lord!" And that's when the song "No Weapon" by Fred Hammond came on the radio and I begin to cry even harder. I felt God washing all my pain, negative feelings and hurt away so that I wouldn't be affected any longer by the words of others. What am I saying?

You might be the mother of 1, 2, 3, 4 or maybe more children, or maybe you're a mother with one child, praying and trusting God for another. Whatever your situation, thank God because some women go to a fertility facility and take shots to become a mother.

Our Children rely on us as parents to love, protect and to care for them; they don't ask to be here. However God sees something in us that says, it's time for me to send this child even if we as parents feel or think we're not ready. Don't let the words and opinions of others cause you to regret having your children, don't give them any power! Believe what God's word says about you and trust His word only!

You can't allow people to put their frustration, fear, and negativity on you because you choose to have a family. Whose life is it anyway? You don't have to allow others to plan your life out for you; it's your life. What you and your husband chose to do that's between you two and God, never allow people to make you regret having your babies or being a mother! God has already equipped and made you ready for this moment; He predestined your life before you ever existed on this earth. He knew I would be the mother of 8, and He knew I would sometimes be affected and hurt by others, but He also knew that I could handle it. He knows that I would be that mother who would inspire and encourage mothers around the world to not allow people to make you feel like you've done something wrong because you chose to have a family. Live your life to the fullest and teach your children about responsibility. Teach them principles like:

- Be a person of your word.
- Live a life that is pleasing and respectful to others.
- Don't allow others to place their guilt, fear and shame on you.
- Reach for the stars.
- Be the best you.
- Always speak by using your voice and not allowing others to be your voice!

As a mother, like I said earlier, it's not easy but it is rewarding. If we train our children in the way that they shall go, they will never depart from the teachings they have been taught!

⏻ Beautifully Restored

Today I have turned my pain into passion by helping young ladies ages 12 – 22 years old, through my organization Fearless Girls Rocks, a community outreach program designed to reach Young Ladies. Just like I was, these girls are facing challenges that can hinder their success and prevent them from pursuing their dreams and goals in life. As a child, I experienced much of the things that young girls are experiencing now: childhood struggles, pain, emptiness and abandonment. I wanted to create a safe place that would allow them to open up and talk about those things and to let them know they have a voice. I want them to know that their environment does not dictate their future!

I believe No One is exempt from the Pain that life gives out. I am committed to empowering and encouraging young ladies to not allow the events of their lives to hold them hostage. I know that my life is a living testimony of total restoration. I am excited about the journey ahead.

My life has taught me some things that I would like to share with you. Doing these things helped me to become the success I am today. I am thankful that as I grew in age, I also grew in wisdom.

1. Avoid negative people... Avoid people who always have a negative thing to say to you. Choose to not engage yourself in conversation with people that always turn things into a negative against you.

2. Surround yourself with positive people... I realized the more I was around the negative, the more I would begin to believe what they would say about me. I gave their words power. One day I woke up and realized I needed to change my environment. I begin to surround myself with people that encouraged and supported my decisions. I identified the positive people in my life and I reallocated my time by being around positivity. I took my power back, by not allowing negative people to scrutinize my choices, life and the decision I chose for me! You can do the same thing; surround the positive and discard the negative people in your life. You will overcome every time, I did!

3. Ask yourself, "is what's being said true or a lie?" At this point, let's take this a little deeper. It comes a time in your life that you just must acknowledge that a lie is a lie. It doesn't matter who is saying it. Even though it was a lie I had to deal with the hurt of it. And ask myself why is this affecting me the way it is? I had to talk myself through each area of the pain that the lie affected and forgive each person who instigated the lie. With the dismissal of the pain, I began to declare the truth concerning my life and choices. Which brings me to the next point.

4. If it's not the truth, then what is true? At this point you have already determined what has been said about you is not true. So, challenge the lies with the Truth. Ask yourself what is true and answer the question. For my situation, the truth was I am married and if my husband and I decide to have more children, that's our choice! It's your choice to make whatever decision you choose for your life. Whatever is true for your situation, that's what you tie your energy into. Live that truth out every day, unhindered by outward influences. Your truth makes you free, it makes you live out your freedom from others.

5. Make the decision to live a life unhindered by what others think or say and daily embrace the truth of that day. Not yesterday's truth and definitely not tomorrows truth.

In taking these steps, you will begin peeling back the layers of pain, loss, anger, bad decisions or whatever layers you have that has held you hostage to those issues. You decide... Yes, you decide to Live a life beautifully restored!!

Where do you find your POWER?

Deep inside my soul, it comes from a seed that was planted by my mother with the scripture that says "For God hath not given us the spirit of fear; but of power, and of love and of sound mind" 2 Timothy 1:7 KJV

Chapter 8

Balance Life in Heels

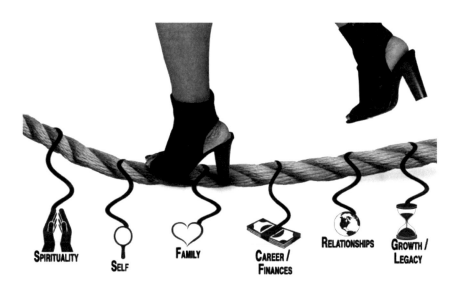

SPIRITUALITY   **SELF**   **FAMILY**   **CAREER / FINANCES**   **RELATIONSHIPS**   **GROWTH / LEGACY**

Superwoman is a myth, a fictional character. There is no cape, bracelet or crown that will help you do things faster, stronger or better. The reality is the closest thing we have here on earth to a superwoman is a powerful woman. A powerful woman is a woman who is not afraid to walk the tightropes of life and figure things out as she goes and as she grows.

As women, we wear many different hats, heels and hearts. No matter your age, career level or bank account balance, learning how to balance it all and create a less stressful life is something many women work to achieve. We are all searching for balance. Some women struggle with being the perfect wife, mom, daughter, friend and student. While others fill their time with work, charity events, volunteering and even over extending their time and energy to people, places and projects that don't line up with their true goals in life. The fact is real balance is a spiritual informed decision and it won't be found in one particular area of your life. It definitely won't be found by over extending or sacrificing yourself for others.

So much has been written about having a balanced life and there are many ways to answer the question; what does having a balanced life mean? Having a balanced life means something different to everyone. There is no right or wrong answer just the right answer for the right person for that stage of their life. For me having a balanced life means I have given my time and energy to the important areas of my life at that moment and at that time. It means that I am at peace with my decisions as a wife, mother, community mom, sister, daughter, aunt, cousin, friend, mentor, youth advocate, community leader, employee, business owner and consultant. Yes, I wear many hats and heels!

Without balance, I would not have been able to survive being a military spouse; moving to a new city, state and even another country every two to three years. Having to start everything over and over again. Knowing how to balance life allowed me to be able to adjust to living in five different states and in Naples, Italy. I was able to balance looking for a new place to call home, searching for a new job, getting my daughter settled into a new school, meeting new friends all while supporting my active duty husband.

Creating this balanced life was not easy nor was it something I started off thinking of in my early stages of marriage or motherhood. I just did things and got them done, not once thinking of how it affected other areas of my life. Sure, I stressed out over work, family, money, and fitness. I over extended myself and put my ambitions on the back burner. Until one day, while stationed in Naples, Italy - I walked into my house and told my husband, "I've had enough and I was tired of being Petty Officers King's wife and Valencia's mom!"

It was at the moment, I realized I had lost myself and my life was out of balance. I had to find myself and redefine who I was and what was important to my spiritual well-being and me. It was at that time I literally sat down and listed the six areas of my life that I felt were out of balance.

- Spirituality
- Self
- Family
- Career
- Relationships
- Growth

What I have come to find out is when these areas of my life are not aligned my purpose and perspective on life is out of balanced. When these areas are not balanced I get moody, irritable, and snappy. I have self-doubt, which leaves me unproductive, and blocks my creative nectars from flowing. When my life is out of balance the essence of whom I am as a powerful woman (power mom) is unhinged. So how do I keep it all together and stay balanced? I'm glad you ask! I stay balanced with prayer and determination.

The first thing is to set viable goals and come to the understanding that having a balanced life starts and ends with YOU. For me, having a balanced life is knowing I have given my all to the priorities in my life at that time and in that moment. For me, learning to create a balanced life came from a place of uncertainty, insecurity and frustration. I was in a sunken place and I had to figure out how to get back to a leveled playing field. So I reached out to other women and I started to analyze what my own power mom did to raise my siblings and I that did or didn't work. Then I made adjustments to fit my lifestyle accordingly.

Do you think it's possible to equally balance your personal, professional and spiritual life? Yes, if you want to fool yourself into thinking you can give equal time across all aspects of your life. If so, my hat and heels go off to you and you should write a book, create a course and teach the rest of us how to spread our time and energy equally. If you are like the rest of us powerful women and are more realistic, then you know that you can't give an "equal" amount of time to each area of your life without something being shortchanged. And that's okay!

If you are like me and you give 100% of what time you have to what you are working on at the moment, then you are on the path to creating a balanced life. The fact of the matter is not all things in life are equal and not all things in life require an equal amount of time. In this lifetime, you will miss appointments, birthdays, date nights, plays, rehearsals, girls' night out, anniversaries and maybe even a championship game or debate contest. It happens. We can't be all things and in all places at one time. The important thing is that you communicate what you can and can't do up front, openly and honestly with the parties involved. Although we are powerful women, we are not perfect!

You may be asking yourself, how do I know if my life is out of balance? To answer that you must ask yourself some tough questions?

Is your marriage in shambles?

Do you have problematic children?

Would you call yourself a workaholic?

Do you feel a lack of spiritual alignment?

Are you burnt out at work, home or school?

Do you feel guilty about where and how you spend your time?

Do you feel physically exhausted, mentally stagnant or find yourself without close relationships?

If you answered yes to any of these questions, your life is probably out of balance.

Now let's discuss what does it mean to be out of balance.

It could mean you don't have stability or harmony in your life. It could mean you are not thinking clear-headed, you are not motivated, you have health concerns, you have financial issues, or you feel a lack of spiritual connection. It could also mean you have relationship issues with your spouse, your children, family and friends. Having an unbalanced life means you are not connected with your church or community.

Learning to balance life is not a one-size fits all and it definitely won't happen overnight. It's a process that takes time, prayer and determination. The first step to learning to balance it all is to self-reflect and get to know yourself, your needs and acknowledging what's important to you and your well-being. This takes me back to the six elements of life that are important to me. In order for me to create the balanced life I have I had to ask myself what are my goals? I had to:

- Determine my priorities
- Make time for myself
- Set goals and create a schedule
- Learn to manage my stress and my procrastination
- Eliminate distractions (projects and people)

Now let's take a closer look at the six elements of my life and how I set goals that helped me balance it all and how setting goals can help you balance it all to!

For starters let me take you on a journey. I will share with you how I created balance in my life using the six elements in the diagram below and what they represent for me in hopes it will help you learn to balance your priorities, your goals and set boundaries.

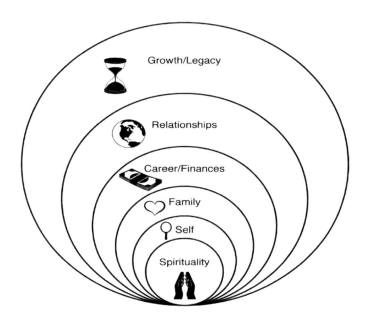

Growth/Legacy

Relationships

Career/Finances

Family

Self

Spirituality

⏻ SPIRITUAL

None of us are exempt from problems; therefore, you must always remember to equip yourself with the armor of spiritual balance. Spirituality is different for everyone. For most, it is the awakening process by which we begin to explore our own being and connection to a higher power. For me, that process is prayer and meditation. When it comes to Spiritual balance in my life, I have prayer warriors and a prayer closet. In this area of life, you need to identify what wakes you up in the morning and give thanks for all that has been given to you.

Learn to think positive, meditate and connect with your soul. The closer you can connect with your soul the closer you can become with God. Having a spiritual relationship with God does not require any special knowledge, degree or sacrifice. Everyone can have a spiritual connection with God. All that is required is desire, dedication and discipline. Reading the bible and other uplifting books on daily basis is a great way to grow spiritually and create a balanced life. Learn to meditate and or quiet your mind. Don't allow external circumstances to decide your internal happiness. Think positive and always be in control of what enters your mind, body and soul.

"But seek ye first the kingdom of God,
and his righteousness, and all these things
shall be added unto you."

Matthew 6:33 KJV

 ## SELF

Balance has to start with you, and taking care of self is the first step. Your emotional, mental and physical well-being should be your top priority. You have to take time for you, yes "Me Time".

You simply cannot accomplish what needs to be accomplished unless you are mentally, physically and spiritually aligned. You need rest, exercise and a balanced diet. Being in good shape mentally and physically increases your tolerance to stress and reduces sick days. Eating right, exercising and getting adequate rest is the best face-lift a woman can have. Numerous studies have shown, staying active on a regular basis, having a regular exercise routine can reduce stress, depression, anxiety, and enables people to better cope with adversity. It will also boost your immune system and keep you out of the doctor's office. Make time in your schedule for the gym, take a walk during lunch, join a fitness group, sports team, boxing club or even a dance class. Sports has always been my thing. I played basketball up to the age of forty-three and I had the opportunity to play overseas at the age of thirty. Fitness has always been a part of my life so why does it have to stop because I got married or had children? Learn to adjust your external needs with you internal desires.

When it comes to taking care of yourself, I want you to find something you enjoy doing and just do it! Taking time to pamper yourself can be as simple as taking a bubble bath, reading a good book with a glass of wine and your favorite music-playing softy in the background. Taking time for yourself could be as simple as getting a facial, pedicure, massage, going bowling or even a girl's night out. A weekend or day trip with just the girls has never done me wrong. Taking care of yourself mentally, physically and emotionally will allow you to stay focused, regroup, self-reflect and reorganize your life. It will allow you to take control of your mind and your decision-making ability. Most importantly, "me time" allows you to empower and re-energize your mind, body and soul.

⏻ FAMILY

When it comes to family, you have to learn to take control of your role as a woman as those roles change. As a spouse, I had to learn to put the needs of my husband before mine. I had to learn to operate as a military spouse and stay out of his career so that our marriage and relationship could flourish. I came to understand no matter how I tried I would never know what its like to put on a uniform that represents honor, devotion and sacrifice. In doing so, it created a mutual respect and understanding for both of us. Staying married for over twenty-five years means I learned to communicate, compromise, and commit with trust, respect and forgiveness. It is very important to recognize that there is a difference between compromising in a relationship or marriage and compromising yourself for a relationship or marriage. The two are not the same.

Just like all relationships, marriage is a two-way street and can be challenging at times. It's up to the two of you to determine what roadblocks to go around and which roadblocks to avoid at all cost. I have this handwritten quote on my bedroom wall that says "Marriage is what you make it, so let's make it together" and I mean every bit of it.

The most important take-away I have for you on how to balance your marriage is to keep family and friends out of your marriage and allow each other to control the factors they bring to the marriage. This applies to dating as well. The roles and rules have not changed, but how those roles are defined have.

Clearly defined roles don't exist anymore and there's no such thing as a perfect family. Leave it to Beaver and The Cosby Show were TV Sitcoms that were very wholesome and groundbreaking, yet they were still unrealistic for the majority of households in America. Parenting in today's world requires flexibility as our ability to juggle competing demands for our time has increased tremendously. You can no longer say "Wait until your father gets home." You'd better deal with it then and now or your child will have moved on to the next ordeal with no sense of consequence and act like it never happen. There are more single mom households than ever before so yes the parenting roles have changed. Moms are taking on the role of breadwinner, caregiver and disciplinarian. If you are the breadwinner be that, if you are the homemaker be that and if you are both well be both to the best of your ability.

When it comes to family and loved ones I had to make clear what my expectations are. No glitz and glamour just plain truth, trust, and I dare you to cross the line. Learn to spend quality time with those who are important to you even if it's to drop them a call to say, "I love you and even though I haven't been around, I still cherish our relationships." A simple phone call or card can go a long way. I am not opposed to reaching out via social media; I just would not make it my primary way of communicating with family. Let your family know where you are in life and how they can be of assistance and how you may be able to help them. You may share planning or attending kids events. You could even do babysitting or weekend swaps that allow you to take a moment for yourself or your relationship.

⏻ CAREER/FINANCES

My mother once told me, "When you know your purpose, you will know your pursuit." As women we work hard for our careers and even harder keeping our families together, and we should not have to choose between the two. When it comes to working, Corporate America wants us to feel guilty about being away from home and when it comes to our children, society wants us to feel guilty about the lack of time spent at home. I have learned that I frankly don't give two cents about what the next person feels about how I run my household or my career. I knew my life was out of balance when I realized I kept separate calendars one for home and one for work, but that changed right around junior high school for my daughter Valencia. I had to learn there is just one me and that one me comes with a family and business take it or leave it. I had to learn to be authentically me and my first priority is and will always be my family. I found it easier to adapt my job/business to my family than my family to my business. Being a Human Resource Consultant has its challenges so I had to show my family exactly what I do. I had to open my work world so that my family understood why I worked late hours, and why I had to be very strict and closed off when it came to my career. Once I did that I was able to stay focused and in the moment, even when that moment was cut short. So let's talk about how do you know if you are out of balance in this area: let's answer these questions.

- Do you keep saying you're overbooked, overwhelmed or overworked?
- Do you feel responsible for saving, investing and spending?
- Do you feel responsible for building wealth and passing it on to future generations?
- Are you out of shape?
- Are you glued to your phone?

If you answered to yes to any of these questions, then your life is probably out of balance. For most people maintaining a healthy work-life balance seems like an impossible goal. Whether you're married with children, a single mom or a woman on a mission; we all juggle heavy workloads from managing family responsibilities, relationships, careers and hobbies. It does not surprise me that the new term "Super Busy" is the way most women describe their day. Being super busy does not mean you were productive. If all you do is put out fires, you are too busy to tend to your own flames.

When you become too busy, you are more likely to miss opportunities that allow you to have creative growth that could lead to successful business and ideas. Allowing unnecessary busyness to creep into your life will create distractions and take you away from what's important and what makes dollars and cents. You have to learn to set boundaries for office, work, family and in my case consulting time. If you have ever gotten to the point where you feel you have to choose between work and family, you've let it get too far out of control and out of balance.

⏻ RELATIONSHIPS

As a relationship expert what I can tell you is appreciation goes a long way. I have been featured on radio shows, as a panelist, speaker, and even a guest on The Dr. Phil Show. I produce and co-host a radio show with a featured segment and PodCast called Ask The Kings with my husband, where we listen and provide relationship advice. So when I use the word "relationships", I am encompassing the various cultural relationships you will encounter in your lifetime both personal and professional. Being a military spouse who has lived in six different states and overseas, means I have entertained and maintained various relationships. Long-term and short-term relationships, good relationships and not so good relationships. I have experienced relationships that are beneficial and relationships that have been a non-factor. The one thing I can say for sure is "all" relationships go through changes, trials and tribulations. The other thing I can say without hesitation or uncertainty is the good news is you get to decide who and what deserves your time and energy! Don't be afraid to remove and replace negative relationships with positives ones. I can't stress it enough when I say - "you control who you let in your circle of life and who you don't." My grandmother Ruby Lee Jackson once told me "there is a reason, a season and a lifetime for every relationship and every relationship has a message or a lesson." I have since then added to that by saying, "the message may not be yours to receive and the lesson may not be yours to learn." With that said, I feel it is very important to take a step back and seriously evaluate your relationships every so often. You have to ask your self how is this relationship, partnership or collaboration making me a better person? I am really putting forth my all and are others benefiting from what I have to give, say or share? Sometimes you have to ask yourself why am I even connected to this relationship in the first place, have I outgrown its purpose? Remember when it comes to relationships and social commitments you have to be honest, be clear and be specific about the expectations and the energy you give them. You need to recognize any differences and acknowledge any miscommunications to reduce negatively, resentment and mistrust. Finally, if the relationship is not working for you - you need to be whiling and able to move on without regret.

 ## LEGACY

Although a financial legacy is holistic, your legacy is not restricted to financial wealth. It's not how much money you've earned or leave behind. It's about values and life lessons. It's about who you are, whom you've touched and the difference you made in the world in which we live. Think about it, you are creating your legacy while you live and by the way you live your life today. Your legacy is about the impact you made on those who've crossed your path. Your legacy will be what your community says about you as a servant of leader, mentor and how to pay-it-forward.

So let's think of ways you can leave a legacy. You can start a scholarship for under-served communities. Helping others is the best way to help yourself. You can write or record a memoir for your children's children, so they truly know your story. Leaving a legacy is about living your life with the thought of how you want to be remembered and planting seeds that grow in times of uncertainty. For me, I pay it forward by lending my time to the YMCA, in school Career Days and volunteering to help women with a second chance at life. I have been on school and business boards of directors offering my area of expertise for the advancement of others.

Remember, no one arrives at success alone so share your knowledge, skills and abilities with someone to empower them and so that they can, in turn, empower others. When thinking about your legacy remember to stay true to yourself, your core- the essence of your being. That's what legacy is all about.

How to balance it all in heels exercise workbook coming spring 2018. For a free downloadable, full-size copy of this worksheet, please visit www.ShirleyWalkerKing.com.

In order to create a Balanced Life You must be ready to take action:

- Assess your life as it is right now.
- Make a conscious decision to be balanced.
- Set goals in every area of importance.
- Be whiling to make adjustments as needed [for you] to balance it all.

Make your list of your top 5 priorities in life right now:

1.
2.
3.
4.
5.

This list may change over time and often and guess what - that's okay!

Now let's evaluate what takes up most of your time and energy that is not a priority in your life.

1.

2.

3.

Can any of these things be eliminated, transferred, or deferred? If so do it, pass it on or let it go. Then you have a better idea of what and who your priorities are and figuring out how to balance it all will come much easier. Stay focused and stay on the offense of your time, your energy your and your strength. I call that Mommy-Tasking. Don't be afraid to ask for help from the people in your circle. As long as the task gets done to the best of your ability and you communicate that to the parties involved you will make it happen. Remember learning to balance it all starts and ends with YOU!

P.S.

"Creating a balanced life is up to you. The goal is to get to a point where you feel good about your decisions and you are in control of your happiness." ~Shirley Walker-King~

Where do you find your POWER?

My power comes from God of course. But also my trials. The more trials I overcome the more power I feel! The more I realize His strength can be my strength. His power can give me power!

Chapter 9

Building Healthy Relationships

When you are a mom, building relationships take on a whole new dynamic and meaning. Your connections now can include the relationships of your children. You become connected to their friends, their friend's parents, teachers, etc. Relationships are a vital part to having a healthy life. The past, present, and future help shape who we are. You can determine a lot from a person's relationship history. Relationships in any stage ranging from passion to friends have the power to enhance or lessen the quality of our lives. We must ensure a healthy structure and balance, or these same relationships can cause heartbreak, pain, and discomfort. Just like anything else, if built on a healthy foundation the structure can last a lifetime.

I know everyone has heard the term of "healthy relationships" over and over again. We have all heard how important they are (myself included). I have read those books, articles, journals, and blogs discussing this at length. I often took nothing away from most of these! Here's why... time! I felt like I didn't have enough time to test the strength and validity of my relationships. I felt like I didn't have time to safeguard and complete a relationship inventory. I was already giving my husband, my three kids and my two jobs my time. When would I have time to sit back and complete a 50-question inventory checklist, like one particular reading was asking me to do? My life was already on overdrive. In order to complete this questionnaire, I had to have a moment of quiet. Quiet times are hard to come by in my home.

My desire is to educate moms not only on how to build a healthy relationship, but mainly how to build a healthy relationship in the confines of a mother's very busy life. It seems like there are countless of things we have to ensure are healthy. If we're married or in a relationship, we have to make sure our partners, child(ren), and parents are healthy, just to name a few. Now, are we supposed to make sure that relationships within those relationships are healthy? I am going to very real and honest with you. YES! Although this does give us another item on our ever-growing to-do list, it is extremely important. Let's look at relationship health the same way we do physical health.

In my private practice, I educate couples on the importance of relationship health. There are countless amounts of time that we spend devoted to diets, meal plans, exercise routines, exercise challenges, doctor appointments and medication. Why? To achieve or get close to optimal physical health. However, relationship health is just as vital as all of the things previously mentioned. Here's why: Think back over your life. Think of your childhood, adolescence, teen years, adulthood, and motherhood. This includes good and bad moments. Now, what made those moments good or bad? For most of us, those moments revolved around a relationship. A relationship with our mother, father, sister, brother, aunts, uncles, grandparents, cousins, friends, teachers, boyfriends, girlfriends, etc... These associations are all around us and some are closer than others. Some were more impactful than others. Nevertheless, they are surrounding and impacting us constantly. So where do we start? We know how crucial relationships are and more importantly how vital healthy ones are, so now what? Now, we start at the foundation. Let's first define what a healthy relationship is. We can't create something if we don't have an idea of what it is or what it's supposed to look like.

A relationship is when two or more people have a connection or bond. It's the way in which two or more concepts, objects, or people are connected. A healthy relationship consists of Mutual Respect, Trust, Forgiveness, Fairness, Honesty, Support, Equality, Effective Communication, Vulnerability, Playfulness and Laughter. These components take effort and will. Now, most relationships will have a combination of these healthy characteristics as well as unhealthy characteristics. Relationships take time and energy to maintain. Building a healthy relationship requires more intentional effort than maintaining. INTENTIONAL EFFORT is the golden ticket and not just ones involving romance. This applies to friendships, family, employment, as well as romantic relationships.

Our goal is to make sure most, if not all, of our relationships are healthy. I know if some of you think the way I do, you'd probably say "well, what if I just keep my closest relationships healthy and just maintain the limited contacted ones?" Mmmmm, because that's kind of like saying "well, how about if only the organs I use most are healthy and the ones I don't use often are just maintained?" In order for a harmonious balancing and functioning body, you need all parts/organs working at their best for optimal health. The same rules apply to your relationships. You don't just want your immediate relationships healthy when you can have all of your relationships in a healthy status. This can lead to a to a more optimal social/relational health.

Healthy relationships are to provide more pleasure and contentment vs. less hurt and anxiety. Notice I used the words "more" and "less" instead of "always" and "never". This is because there will still be worry, hurt, stress, and/or anxiety, but they will appear less in frequency in a healthier relationship. When you have two separate individuals bonding together in whatever matter or dynamic, there is going to be some friction. The objective is to prevent persistent friction and exposure to stressors. Life is stressful enough as a mom. A healthy relationship consists of some key components listed below.

⏻ Self Esteem

Having a good self-esteem keeps balance. It keeps you from being taken advantage of, being dependent, or co-dependent. Self-esteem keeps your identity separate from the relationship, sustaining you as an individual. Having low esteem can alter your perception and your thought processes. If you feel like you are unworthy, you'll doubt others interest in you and second guess yourself. Why would they want to be friends with me? Why do they want to be in a relationship with me? What makes me so special? Why me and not her? If you feel this way about yourself and think this way about yourself long enough, it's only a matter of time before you start to behave in a manner that is reflective of those thoughts. You may start to unintentionally seek and accept relationships where you are mistreated and mishandled in a manner that is reflective of those negative thoughts and feelings. You may also damage positive relationships if you feel undeserving. Everyone suffers from low self-esteem every now and again. Things like losing a job, change in appearance, weight gain/weight loss or gossipers can trigger moments of low self-esteem. Frequency and duration of low self-esteem moments determine the severity. Unlike low self-esteem, healthy levels of self-esteem creates confident and healthy attachments.

Ok, so I've told you what low self-esteem is and how it impacts relationships. We've discussed the benefits of having a high, healthy self-esteem in building a strong relationship. If you're like me, you're saying, "Well thank you for this information, but how do I create or keep high self-esteem?" Good question. Here are some ways to help create or increase your self-esteem:

1) STOP comparing yourself to other moms, to other wives, to other girlfriends, or even comparing yourself to the ex-partners of your spouse. You are beautifully and wonderfully made. Also keep in mind you are comparing yourself to an image. These people whom we are comparing

ourselves to may be displaying an image. We have no idea what happens behind their doors. We have no idea what is at their core. We may be comparing ourselves to a fictional character or mirage. Compare yourself to yourself! Know that you are enough and worthy. There is nothing that you could have done, there is nothing that you could have said, and there is nothing that you could have experienced to make you unworthy of healthy, solid, and loving relationships.

2) You are perfectly imperfect. STOP striving for perfection. There is no such thing as perfection for us humans. If you use perfection as your finish line or mile marker you will set yourself up for failure. Many moms strive to be the perfect mother. Trying to give our kids just enough love, just enough structure, just enough freedom with just enough supervision, just enough play with just enough learning. Constantly making sure the scales don't tip too much in either direction. In an attempt for perfect balance, this becomes exhausting and draining. In order to have and keep high self-esteem, we need to be at our best mentally and physically.

3) STOP beating yourself up. This is another favorite we moms like to dive into. Beating ourselves up if we have missed a homework deadline, science project, dance recital, sports practice, PTA meeting, Field trip, and whatever else we have on this buffet plate. It's ok to drop that ball. I mean look at all the items we're juggling. We're bound to drop 1, 2, or heck even 3. But you know the secret.... IT'S OK! It's ok if our house isn't clean. It's ok if the garbage isn't taken out and the house smells like the salmon you made two nights. It's ok if you missed a homework assignment. The good news

is, everyone will survive. Spend less time beating yourself up and more time praising yourself. Which leads me to the next point.

4) Uplifting and praising your efforts. Many times, we don't praise our efforts. We may miss the mark on some of the items stated above. We get so caught up in beating ourselves that we ignore the efforts. Although, you and I have never met. I know for a fact that you put great effort into being a mom/ wife/ girlfriend/ friend. Praise the effort you put forth. We conquer a lot on very little sleep and food. Stop right now and take a moment to praise your efforts. Even reading this book is an effort to self-improve. If you won't praise yourself. Let me start first... "You are such a great mom. You love your kids and it shows. You love them so selflessly." Don't worry if you forget an errand or chore. Don't worry if you missed/forgot an appointment. Don't worry if you didn't buy the right snack. Don't worry if you submitted the field trip money and permission slip late. You STILL woke up this morning with a long to do list and I'm sure you tackled most of it. You may not have felt appreciated today or heard a thank you. So, I say Thank you for your effort. I appreciate your sacrifice and dedication.

⏻ Trust

Trust is vital in every relationship. Trust is something we all know is needed and required. We hear this almost everywhere and from everyone. As frequent and as popular as it is, many of us battle with trust. This goes for me as well. I admit there are things and areas that I struggle to have trust in and still do. I know from experience how hard it is.

We struggle with trust as a result of different causes. From different past or even current experiences.

Let's talk about exactly what trust is and means. Trust means that you can let your guard down, you are assured, and you feel protected. You believe what your partner or friend tells you is the truth. You are confident that their answers are truthful. Trust prevents doubt. It limits questions like: Are they really where they say they are? Do they mean what they say? Will they hurt me? Will they disappointment? Do I want to start over? You can drive yourself crazy with the possibilities. You can also drive the other person crazy. This could create a wedge and web of distrust. It will even shift your conversations. Instead of asking healthy questions, you begin to interrogate with questions motivated from fear and distrust.

Distrust and fear are two different things, but they go hand in hand. What's the driving force behind mistrust? FEAR! Fear of being hurt, fear of being lied to, just fear of the unknown. Fear can hinder you from enjoying your relationship and your ability to fully connect with another person.

Now let's see how we can apply and/or create trust for our relationships. This might sound crazy but the key to trust is first trusting yourself. Trust your instinct, gut, intuition, and wisdom. Don't go against your better judgment. More often than not our instinct tells us when something is wrong or right. We then chose to ignore it and push forward. If you get that tugging in your Spirit, heart, and/or gut, Go with it. This thermometer can help to gauge trust in any relationship. Trust that you are worthy enough to demand honesty. Trust you are worthy of the truth and rightfully so, deserving of it.

If you have a relationship or friendship and there is mistrust, it's not too late to rebuild trust. Start with being open and transparent about vulnerabilities. Be honest with the other person and YOURSELF. Be vocal and don't hide what your feelings are. Speaking of being vocal, let's dive into that. Sometimes being vocal isn't always a good thing. It depends on your delivery. It's vital to talk about the trust issues with the appropriate delivery. So, let's discuss that further. The biggest key to building a healthy relationship is COMMUNICATION!

⏻ Communication

Communication is the most crucial component in building and maintaining a healthy relationship. Be open, speak, and listen. People often only think of communicating as speaking. However, a large part of communication is listening. What I frequently come across with the couples that I counsel is that often times, they don't really listen to the other partner. Instead, they are just waiting for their time to reply. Have you ever heard that saying, "we have two ears and one mouth, so we can listen twice as much?" This is a very accurate statement. Listen with your heart and not your head. Hear the persons heart behind what they are speaking. Other than listening, what does effective communication look like:

1) Face to Face: Face to Face communication is always best. In recent years, we have cut face to face communication down tremendously. Replaced by Social Media, Text Messages, Emails, Instant Messengers, and even phone calls are less frequent. These methods can lead

to misinterpreted or misconstrued expressions. Talking in person can lessen miscommunication. Now, if you are not a very vocal person or find that expressing yourself makes you uncomfortable, then try to write out your feelings and thoughts. Then read them face to face to the intended party. Still creating an opportunity to look in one another's face and into one their eyes. This allows you not only to hear what the person is saying but also see their expressions when they are saying it. You can tell a lot by looking at someone directly in their face and in their eyes.

2) Source and Sound: Source and Sound means where are we talking from. What is the source of our words. Are we speaking from elevated emotions, anger, frustration, disappointment, or hurt? When we are speaking from these places you better believe more than likely the words spoken won't be pleasant. They may accompany pointed fingers, tearing down, and/or intimidation. The other part of Source and Sound is Sound. Meaning our tone of voice. Aggressive, loud, and stern tones can make the other person not want to listen and communicate with you. We don't want the other person to shut down nor do we want to shut down. The goal is to express oneself and be receptive to the other's perspective or point of view. To review, keep a calm and respectful tone and make sure that you are not speaking from elevated emotions. If so, calm down. Its ok to take a moment before having a conversation to calm down and gather your thoughts.

3) Stay in The Present: Ladies, we are notorious for bringing up past things, past transgressions, and past

incidents into the current. Part of effective communication is staying on topic. We are known for "bringing up old stuff" as the saying goes. Things that we feel are relevant, but truly has nothing to do with the current, leave it in the past. Stay on the current topic, on the current conversation, and the current time.

4) Reflecting: Reflecting is basically summarizing and reviewing what was said and what was felt during a conversation. The reason for reflecting is to show the other person or persons that you have "heard" what they were saying. Showing that you are trying to understand.

5) Body Language: Communication is not just verbal. Our body language is sometimes louder than our verbal language. Be mindful of your body language and personal space. Are you near the person's face when you're talking, invading their personal space? Do you use your hands often? Do you roll your eyes? Do you pump your chest up? Do you punch the air? Do you make a fist? Do you clap your hands? Do you snap your fingers? Do you put your hands on your hips? Do you put your hands or fingers in the other person's personal space? All of these can be interpreted as aggressive body language.   Be mindful of not only the words you say but the manner in which they are delivered. If someone is feeling attacked they are not going to be receptive.   Take body language inventory and assessment. For some of us our body reveals what we are trying to mask. Even when our verbal communication says one thing, our body language can say something totally different. If you're anything like me, I definitely have to monitor and be mindful of my hand

movements. We want to make sure that all parties involved are receptive to what's being said and have an open mind and heart.

Forgiveness

Forgiveness is truly a gift. It's a gift to be forgiven and a gift to know how to forgive. The question is how do you forgive? Forgiveness takes a combination of things to achieve. In order to truly forgive you need to have a level of empathy, understanding, grace, and mercy. You will also need to overlook the transgression or mistake. In a relationship, there are going to be many mistakes some intentional and some not intentional. There will be mistakes made on both sides. So, there will be times when we need to forgive and there will be times where you will need to be forgiven. It takes great strength to forgive someone who has hurt or wronged you. We often feel like forgiving someone makes us gullible or foolish by giving someone another chance. Giving them another chance also means leaving us open for the possibility of another disappointment. Forgiveness can be risky. Forgiveness doesn't mean you are not entitled to feel a certain way or that you are saying what the person has done is ok or acceptable. Forgiveness means you are taking or accepting the experience of what was done and moving on to resolve it. You have accepted also how you felt and how you responded. You don't even need the other person involved in order to forgive. Forgiveness is not about the other person. It's about YOU. It's for YOU to heal.

Forgiveness will take time especially at first. Those feelings of anger, hurt, and disappointment may be too fresh, too deep, and too new. After some time do a self-assessment and see where you are with these feelings. Once you have had time to sort out those feelings, express your anger, and free your pain, you can then start to forgive. Forgiving gives you a freedom. You're no longer held captive to your hurt, harm, disappointment, and anger.

Now as we close out this chapter, I've saved the most crucial element to building a healthy relationship for last. You cannot have any of the other parts without this. This component sets the foundation for everything we have gone through this far. Are you ready? Yes, ok let's go!!!

Assess Your Relationship with Yourself

As moms you already know how much time and energy we put into everyone else except who? You! We are last after everything and everyone. We give our kids the very best of us. Which is great! However, what does your best look like. Could it be better? Could you be better? Have you focused on your relationship with yourself lately or at all? If so, how strong is that foundation? So, let's quickly review the topics we discussed but now let's apply them to ourselves.

Self-Esteem: Have you assessed your self-esteem lately? Our self-esteem can definitely be altered after having children. Most of our bodies have now transformed and some new additions have been added to our frame after birthing these new additions. It's perfectly normal for your self-esteem to be altered but not plummet. If it has flat lined, let's revive it, by reviving you. Let's get back to the things that made you feel good about you. Whether it's getting back into make-up, getting your hair done, manicures/pedicures, going to the gym, playing sports, painting, establishing a new wardrobe, affirmations, posting love notes to yourself, whatever makes you feel good. Do it!

Trust: Trust yourself and your instinct. For example, listening to your body. There are plenty of times where my body is telling me to stop and take a moment. But, I push past it, keep moving, and hustling. Later, I end up paying for that decision. I'll come down with a cold or flu. Overexerting your body can weaken your immune system. Now instead of taking a 1-2-hour nap to rest, now I'm losing 1-2 days in bed sick. I didn't trust me, my instinct.

Communication: Have you had time to communicate with you today? Meaning, time to gather your thoughts? Heck to even just finish your thoughts? Time to pray, journal, and communicate your thoughts/feelings. Remember in the beginning of this chapter I talked about us being so busy that we don't have any time to complete an inventory. We must make that time!! Please find the time. Your quiet time is when you complete a self-assessment of what is missing or needed. Do you need more time to read, exercise, sleep, hang out with friends, etc.? It doesn't have to be long periods of time. But you must find the time. My time is usually in the car while running errands or traveling to and from work.

Self-talk is another important way to communicate with you. It's just what it sounds like... talking to yourself. You can tell yourself how good of a mother, wife, girlfriend, sister, daughter, aunt, niece, or friend you are. Communicate with yourself if you begin to become stressed or overwhelmed. Communicate and speak scriptures or affirmations to yourself. I instruct you to use self-talk when your negative thoughts start to get too loud or too convincing. Self-talk with positive affirmations will combat and override the negative.

Forgiveness: Do you know it's easier to forgive others than it is to forgive ourselves? I found with myself as well as my clients that we can forgive others way before we forgive ourselves. We hold ourselves in bondage and repeatedly punish ourselves. As moms, I know I'm not the only one that has beaten myself up if I forgot the kid's school project due date, doctor's appointment, permissions slips, lunch money, homework, Parent/Teacher conference, or open house. At first, I feel embarrassed because now I have to admit to the teacher or whomever that I dropped the ball on something. Then I feel guilty. How could I have done this? What was I thinking? Then I implement Self-talk and say "Ummm maybe I was thinking about the hundreds of other things due that day. This will be ok".

Transparency Moment: One day I was in such a rush that I actually had to look in the rearview mirror and count my kids to make sure I picked all of them up. I was fearful that I might have forgotten to pick up one of my kids. What kind of mother would I be if I forgot one of my kids?

Now, I have never forgotten to pick them up (knock on wood), but I know moms who have. It happens!!! You may have swapped with your partner and now instead of dropping them off you are picking them up. That day you might have forgotten that you are now picking the kids up. Maybe, you didn't read an email or text message in its entirety and missed the part about practice being cancelled. Now the kids have to be picked up right after school. Whatever the reason may be things like this happen and will continue to happen. But oh, how we beat ourselves up about it. We ponder on that one dropped ball over and over for days, weeks, even months. Forgive yourself. Mistakes happen, and life happens. We are only human. We are only one person. Even with the support of spouses, partners, family, or friends, it's still A LOT of work being a mother. Give the gift of forgiveness to yourself. See how much of the weight falls off your back, shoulders, heart and mind when you do. You are giving your family your very best. Now give you, your very best as well.

If these steps are utilized, you will be on your way to building a healthy relationship. Just remember it does take work, time, and effort in building anything the strong healthy way. Remember, everything that is built strong has a greater potential to last long.

Meet: Katrina Hudson

Where do you find your POWER?

I find my power through God. There is no way for me to endure the things which I've experienced without calling on the power and strength of God.

Chapter 10

Against All Odds

When it was impressed upon me to tell my story, I was a bit hesitant. In the past years, my life has changed in so many ways for the better, that sometimes I don't want to think about the choices that I made when I was younger. The truth is, we all have things hidden in our closets that we aren't comfortable sharing, in fear of the judgment we'll face from of others. But like the saying goes, *"People in glass houses, shouldn't throw stones."* I know that it's finally time for me tell my story…the good, the bad and the ugly.

I have overcome bad relationships, children with multiple fathers and being homeless… but, that's just part of my story. I have been able to minister to countless of lives of women and help hurting people turn their lives around. No one is exempt from hard times. No one is exempt from making bad choices. I am thankful to God that I have overcome every storm. I have Won… Against all of the Odds

I had been in a relationship for about 10 years with a man I felt I was in love with. Although we shared a beautiful daughter together, I had to realize that I could no longer stay in a relationship filled with cheating, lies and deceit. When people would see me, they figured I had it all together. That was the farthest thing from the truth. I was hurting deep inside. I hid it well. The brokenness that I never healed I from in my childhood spilled over into my adult life and it left me clueless as to who I really was. I did a very good job in covering up my scars. I would find myself sitting in the darkness trying to figure out where I was, and what was this thing that continued to happen to me.

As a young child, we are taught that every girl is to be married, have children and take care of your home (*and in that order*). The thing I struggled with is why we weren't taught how to take care of our emotional and mental well-being. No one warned me when I grew up into a young woman, life would hurt. No one told me to be careful of whom I gave my heart to because that person might not be qualified to take care of it. I was not a bitter woman, but I was a lost woman. I was a confused woman.

Everything I was taught about love and relationships was a lie. I was only exposed to the things my women friends wanted others to see. It was a false reality of what was going on behind their closed doors. I would ask questions in my mind like, *How did they become so happy? How did she get so lucky to have a loving caring man like that?* Unbeknownst to me, she was also abused and broken. She covered up her scars very well. She hid behind her story in fear of exposing the truth, like so many us are guilty of. Well, how was I supposed to recognize what wasn't real when I had no clue what real was? There were too many women around me wearing the cover up sign, just like I was wearing mine. Not knowing who I was, caused me to make some bad choices early on in my life.

I was 20 years old when I had my first child. Even though I had no clue what motherhood was all about, I longed to be a mother. My son brought so much joy to my heart. He had filled a void in me that I was missing so desperately. I needed someone that I could love, and they would love me back. It felt good to see him look at me without judging me. But as time went on I started noticing something was still missing. The love from my son was the best thing ever, but I was longing for companionship. I was looking for someone other than my son to love me.

My son's father and I broke up before he was born, because of his infidelity while I was pregnant. After our relationship ended, I started spiraling out of control dealing with other men. By the time my son turned one, I had started dating "the love of my life" (*so I had thought*). He was a charmer. He pulled out all the stops for me. He made me feel special. I thought this is it. This is what I had been looking for. I had no idea the whirlwind I would experience when I would later find out he had twins from another woman, on the way. I couldn't believe this was happening again. This was one more man to come into my life and ultimately take my heart and destroy it. I was crushed... but I couldn't let go. I was broken and in love. I was torn between what I wanted and what I needed, and I allowed him to feed me lies because I didn't want to be without him. I accepted the cheating. I accepted the lies. It was easier to deal with that than the truth. I didn't want to face the truth because it meant I would have to face me. I wasn't ready to face me; I wasn't equipped for it. I made a toxic life decision from a dark place. He offered me a temporary love that I mistook as a permanent love. This may sound crazy, but I was so bad off I took on the attitude that I didn't care what other woman was involved in his life, as long as he took care of me and didn't leave me. I was willing to play Russian Roulette with my life.

After about two years of dating him I became pregnant, and during the pregnancy, we broke up. It was hard for me, I allowed the emotions to get the best of me, and I became a high-risk pregnancy and ended up in the hospital. He didn't show up one time. It was a painful lesson, but I pressed on. We slowly started drifted apart. I would continue to see him from time to time, hoping we could rekindle what we once had. Being heart-broken is like a sickness that eats at you constantly. If you never face your truth, you will repeat it over and over again. And I did.

A few months after my daughter was born we eventually reunited. Things were good. He proposed to me and even helped me to purchase a house. Life was finally looking up for a while, but eventually the drama started up again. I was tired. Living in a constant state of brokenness was wearing me down in ways I couldn't describe. I remember crying

164

over him so badly that I had to call out to God and ask him to please take that type of love I had for this man away from me. It wasn't normal. It had me doing things that I knew I shouldn't do, like leaving my then two children (Ages 6 and 2) at home by themselves at 2:00 in the morning, while I went to search high and low for him. *What was wrong with me? Why was I accepting a man treating me like this? Why can't I tell him no?* These were questions that constantly surfaced in my mind.

Quite honestly, I had never dealt with the brokenness from my childhood and I reopened the wombs, constantly taking the broken pieces as they fell out of my closet, placing them back in so no one else would recognize it. The God in me was saying, *girl you better get your life together* but the wounded side of me, the ugly side was saying *No! You go wreak havoc.* So, guess what I did? I went and wreaked havoc. I started going over to his house where he lived with his mom and started fights with family members because they too were a part of his lies and deceit. I threw his clothes out on the front lawn and made him give me back my key. I even started having an affair with another man. I went as far as to drive by his house day and night to see if I was going to catch him in the act. Ladies I was out of control. I concluded that I could not stay in the madness that I had so openly contributed to in my life. God was showing me signs every time I cried out, but I ignored them all. We don't listen when God is speaking and then we ask God why he allowed things to happen to us. I had to start taking responsibility for my actions.

I was a Correctional Officer in my early 20's. I was a young and vibrant mother of 2 at the time. I was a homeowner and I was feeling really proud of myself for accomplishing so much at a young age. No one knew the darkness I carried on the inside. I was hurting so bad and I wanted the pain to stop. On top of all the things I was going through, my son started acting out because he wanted to see his father. Unfortunately, my son's father had his own demons that were surfacing, and I started finding out things about him I never knew. Secrets that could bring harm to me and my children. I couldn't allow my son to fall victim to his father's bad choices. I made a promise to God that if he continued to give me breath in my body, I would not allow my son to take the same path his dad took. I was not only fighting for my survival but the survival of my children. I started going to bible study trying to get to know God. I knew of him. I always talked to him since I was a little girl, but I didn't know him intimately. I was finally starting to regain focus.

Mr. Wrong

Mr. Wrong couldn't have been at the workplace for very long before I first noticed him. He was tall, dark, handsome and very charming. The timing couldn't have been worst. I was just starting my journey as a young Christian seeking God in a way that was truly consuming my attention. Unfortunately, it didn't take very long me to lose focus. When he entered the room, it was like time just stood still. The strangest thing was we had never had one conversation yet, I was drawn to him and I had no explanation for it. There was something uniquely special about him. I tried to fight what I was feeling, but the more I fought the more my feelings grew.

Eventually, we started having conversations. I mean we had no choice, he was one of my superiors. After working with him for a couple of weeks I started to let my guard down. One day *Mr. Wrong* decided to take a bold approach and he shared with my supervisor his interest in me. Though my spirit was telling me no, my feelings were saying go for it. Well, needless to say my feelings won the battle and we started dating.

Red Flags

It wasn't long before I fell in love with this man. The red flags were waving all around my head as bright as can be, telling me to run away, but I put my blockers on as if I didn't see them. Unaware of the brokenness inside of me, I had attracted another man that wasn't fit or deserving of my love. I was just excited about the thrill of the work relationship. The entire experience was new for me. I had never dated anyone I worked with before. It was fun, daring and enticing. I was experiencing a side of me I never tapped into before. I felt alive again. Mr. Wrong was legally separated from his wife, but he was still married… I knew the relationship was not right for me, but I did not care. I couldn't help myself. I didn't want to help myself. He had me hooked. I was weak and vulnerable, and I opened myself up to him. How did I get there? I don't know, but life for me was about to turn for the worse.

I began to neglect my spiritual GPS ignoring the warning signs that were there signaling me about the danger ahead. I wasn't dating Mr. Wrong for long before I found out that I was pregnant. *What have I done? This makes baby daddy number 3. Why me?! Why him?! God, why did you allow this to happen to me?!* There I was again, blaming God for another bad choice I had made. Isn't it funny how we continue to blame God for our screw ups or mistakes? He says we have freedom of choice. I mean the choice was mine, granted it wasn't the right one, but it was mine. I did not want to have a baby with this man because he was still married. He was separated from his wife, but he was still married, at least that was the story I got. It still did not sit well with me because he had ties to someone else. I was a-risk pregnancy so not only did being pregnant put me in a state of depression, but being high-risk was no jog around the park either. I had just landed a new job set to begin within 2 weeks at another facility. This was an increase in pay for me which came with better benefits. I didn't know how this would play out. But I needed to take the new position. The pregnancy was nerve-wrecking, and my new job was on the line. I had to choose wisely.

I was not excited about being pregnant. Quite honestly, I did not want my baby. I didn't want to entertain the thought of having an abortion either. I had to let him know what was going on. I called to inform Mr. Wrong of the news that he was going to be a daddy. He was on his way to visit his estranged wife and daughter at the time. As I told him the news he began to break down and cry. *Wait a minute; you don't get to break down and cry*, I thought to myself, *Why are you crying?* I became angry with him because in my mind he didn't deserve to have a moment! Well, he cried, and he cried some more. Suddenly, his phone dropped...*Dead silence. What had I just experienced? Did he hang up the phone on me?*

There was no more communication for the whole weekend. Part of me thought he had done something stupid. I had no other way to contact him until I returned to work. When I arrived at work that Monday, I headed straight for his sidekick friend to talk. I needed to get some answers. I informed his friend of the events that had taken place. I just knew that he had already told him, they shared all their deepest secrets, but to my surprise, he had no clue. Mr. Wrong eventually showed up at work as if the whole ordeal over the weekend had never happened. It was like dealing with Dr. Jekyll and Mr. Hyde. Nevertheless, he came in sat me down and proceeded to pour out his heart to me and ensured me that he would take care of his responsibility. I didn't really believe him, but what other choice did I have?

⏻ Sick and Pregnant

This new pregnancy was difficult. I was constantly sick. I was carrying the baby low and to make matters worse; I was back and forth with doctor's visits. But I had to keep things moving; I had a mortgage, a brand-new car, and 2 children in private school. I had to do what a mother had to do. My headspace was totally messed up. I was still trying to process the whole pregnancy thing. I could not get into a happy place. However, Mr. Wrong made good on his word and he was there every step of the way. Forcing me to go to the store to pick up food to eat, helping with my other children ensuring clothing was ready for school, and that they also had what they needed. But as time went by my resentment grew. I just could not come to terms with this new blessing. Oddly enough, I never viewed the pregnancy as a blessing but punishment for my wrongdoing. I thank God for my blessings now, but I couldn't accept it then.

When I reached 6 months pregnant, more skeletons started rattling at my door. I received notice from my old supervisor, who still worked with Mr. Wrong that he had a fling going on with the new switchboard operator. *Say What?* Now this was too much to process. I lost it! I was livid! I contacted Mr. Wrong to confront him about the rumors I had heard. He tried to cover himself though I wasn't buying it. Something wasn't right in my spirit. I felt myself slipping into darkness more and more until I felt like life didn't matter anymore. I continued to be sick and have more doctors' visits and emergency room visits. I was grateful to have a Lieutenant that was caring and understanding of what I was going through. My mother and I were fighting all the time. She was upset that I took time with my other two children and shopped for them, but I refused to pick up one thing for the child that was on the way. I couldn't come to grips with it. I tried. Honestly, I did. I ended up in the ER with Braxton Hicks contractions more times than I could count. I began to feel sorry for the way I was treating my unborn child. I prayed to God to forgive me. I didn't want to lose my baby. Everything around me was falling apart. I had lost sight of who I was. Those skeletons had a job to do and they did it well. They set out to take me out and they almost did. But I learned later down the line when your steps are ordered by God and He has His hands on you nothing can touch you. I was destined for something greater.

It would take heartache, pain and suicide contemplation to get me to the place God needed me to be. Time was winding down for me to have my baby. I continued to prepare for her arrival. Three and a half weeks left to go, and my water broke, I ended up in the hospital early. My mother stayed with me through it all. My good friend finally made contact with Mr. Wrong and informed him the baby had arrived. He didn't visit us at the hospital. His excuse was, "he was new to the area and he didn't know his way around," so he chose not to come. I didn't care at that point. I had this new baby and though I was grateful I was dying inside.

After giving birth to my baby girl, I found it very difficult to bond with her. I became weaker and more confused than ever before. I didn't the have time or energy for the relationship with Mr. Wrong anymore. Something was happening on the inside and I couldn't explain it, I didn't feel like myself. It was like the storm had taken on a mind of its own. The darkness was taking over me to the point I felt that spiritually I was slipping into a coma. I didn't want to hear any more. My soul was crying out Lord how much more can I take? There was no fight left in me. I got to the point that I didn't care what he did. I was broken beyond repair and I just wanted it all to go away. I had no help with my children anymore I realized there was so much more Mr. Wrong was hiding but it would take a few more years before it would come to light.

A Silent Cry for Help

I was slipping away, and I needed help. My best friend was there as a shoulder to cry on, but she couldn't understand the changes I was going through. I didn't even understand them. I had no clue that I was on a spiritual journey. But for the time being, I had to keep up with the facade. I mean I couldn't dare allow others to see what I was dealing with. How would I look? I have fallen and can't get up or S.O.S. send help? I was silently dying inside but pride kept me from reaching out and asking for help. As time went by and I settled into motherhood for the third time, I was struggling emotionally. Trying to adjust to being the mother of a newborn baby again was a challenge. I was silently suffocating. I was being called away from my new job often to take baby girl to the Emergency Room or to the doctor's office. She was always sick and she cried all the time. She never slept which caused me not to rest. *My God, what was happening?* I was breaking down in ways no one could understand. I was deteriorating, and I couldn't do anything about it. I was a hot broken mess. I had more broken pieces added on to the broken pieces I had attempted to hide for years.

I was finding myself dealing with a sick child by myself. Baby girl was six months old when I begin to pray to God to remove this man from my life. The tears were running down my face. I had to go into my hiding closet. I couldn't let anyone see me like that, especially my children. I needed

172

the pain to stop. My heart felt like it wanted to give out. Wait! Was, I having a heart attack? I couldn't discern what it was, but it hurt like hell!! After days and weeks of crying out to God, Mr. Wrong and I parted ways.

By the time my baby girl was two years old, I was so depressed it would hurt to go to work. My mind was messed up. I worked with criminals and I had to be on high alert at all times. I wasn't able to be alert considering my situation; I was putting myself and co-worker's lives at risk. My daughter was scheduled to have her first surgery and I did not go to work for a week. I didn't care whether I had a job or not. I was promised a shift change to be able to care for my sick daughter, but it never happened, and it pushed me over the edge and I resigned. At the time I had no idea that I was experiencing postpartum depression. I was on top of the world at age 24 owning my own house, new car, money in the bank, and kids in private school and by 32 years old I had lost it all. I couldn't process what was happening to me. I recognized that God was somehow there in the midst of my pain, hurt, uncertainty, beat downs and brokenness.

⏻ My Truth

My truth is I was beaten spiritually, physically and mentally beyond recognition and I no longer wanted to indulge in life any longer. I ended up in my living room having what felt like labor pain, but I wasn't pregnant. So how on earth could this be happening?! I was experiencing spiritual labor pains. I was purging from all of the hurt. I was ready to end life as I had known it. The mind is a battlefield and there was a war going on inside of me. I heard God ask me "if you ball up and die who is going to take care of your children like you?" Parts of my heart started tearing. "There is no one to cover them and pray for them like you." The Holy Spirit continued to talk to me about my children. He began to tell me how much they needed me. He also bought to my remembrance a promise I had made to God. I told God when I was young if he would just keep me while I was out in the world I would give my life over to him. He told me he had given me enough time and he had to shut me down to get my attention. It was like no other experience I had in my life. God showed me that he loved me enough to show his Grace and Mercy upon my life. He told me I wouldn't understand the journey I was about to embark on, but there was work for me to do. I gained my strength to continue to fight for my life and my children's lives. I had won the fight to live.

When I reflect on my journey and where I am today, I am excited about my future. In the past years I have been able to turn my life around. I am no longer the woman that allows men to take advantage of her. I am no longer the victim, allowing anyone to come in and out of my life just for companionship. I am happy with the woman I've become. It was not always easy to start over again, but it was worth it. Every day is a new day. Every day I experience a new freedom. If you have ever found yourself in an unhealthy relationship, then you know how hurtful and long the healing process can seem to be. But one thing I am clear about is that I am an overcomer and so are you. I would like to leave you with some of the things that helped me along my journey. I hope they also can help you on your journey.

1. Do not exchange your value for less than what you are worth. You are the only one that can dictate who is allowed to take up residence in your space. The same way you control the temperature in your house is the same way you control the energy around you.

2. Spend some time getting to know you. This is the time you seek God and ask him to reveal you to you. Be ready for the real you because it can be ugly, but that's ok. It is necessary for your healing. It will allow you to embrace who you are and also to address why you accepted certain things within your relationships.

3. Learn how to be by yourself. Often times I found myself needing to have a man in my life. I had no clue as to what it was like to be without one. If you don't take this time alone, you will never be able to heal or have time to figure out what went wrong.

4. Love you for who you are. The good, the bad and the ugly. Whatever needs to be changed you work on it one step at a time. No one said you were perfect. DO NOT allow anyone to put a label on you.

5. Give yourself a break. It's ok to make mistakes but you cannot continue to do it over and over again because you will find yourself back in the saga again.

6. Always keep a journal to write down your thoughts. You never know what God may lead you to do. As this is one the best therapies I've ever had. You need an outlet and sometimes your family or friends may not be able to be that outlet you need. Take time out to re-read what you wrote in your journal. You will be surprised what it reveals about you.

Despite everything I went through, I knew I was destined for something greater than myself. Nothing could have prepared me for the journey I had to take to take. It was mine and mine alone. Oddly enough, I am thankful for the journey. I am thankful that today my beautiful baby girl is a healthy growing teenager.

I must admit I used to be afraid of actually succeeding. Sometimes we don't prepare for success, but we always prepare for failure. It's time we start thinking differently and be willing to walk out our journey alone. If I was able to make it out on the other side, with my struggles, then you can do it too. If you have dreams of being a Mompreneur take steps and strive for it. Stop being so hard on yourself, and surround yourself with like-minded people. I was taught to take baby steps. This scripture was embedded in my head.

Habakkuk 2:2-3, "Write the vision and make it plain on tablets, that he may run who reads it. For the vision is yet for an appointed time; But at the end it will speak, and it will not lie. Though it tarries, wait for it because it will surely come, it will not tarry."

Let this be your motivation for taking that leap. Start writing down your goals. We won't always get it right. But we owe it to ourselves to pursue those gifts that God has given us. Find you some "me" time. Look for scriptures about faith and encouragement. Write them on a sticky note and keep them in front of you. I promise you it will all be worth it in the end.

Meet: Anita Bowman Roussel

Interview Questions:

Any power that I have comes from my faith. I profess Jesus Christ as my Lord and Savior. It is in Him and His Word that I find my purpose, hope, help, guidance and strength. It is in Him that I have persistence, can overcome, win, empower and find restoration. I have also found power in learning how others have overcome or in seeing what others have done. Because if it has been done, then it can be done again.

Chapter 11

One Powerful Secret from One Mom to Another

Contentment - Anticipating the Next Season without Guilt

⏻   The Question That Almost Caused an Eruption

"How does it feel to have it all?" was the question from the young woman that sat before me in my living room. She was a late twenty-something professional that had chosen to join our Friday night home Bible study led by my husband and myself. I was so happy that she had joined but equally surprised that she had stayed. Although our group was open to married couples and singles, the dynamics were such that we were mostly a group of couples with children. And yet, this beautiful young woman that I will call Lena, seemed to enjoy being with us, even though we met on Friday nights, and even with the constant noise of our children.

I suspect that Lena was ready for her season of singleness to end and that was one reason she did not mind our group. She could study what she was hoping to get herself into, that of marriage and motherhood. She even babysat at our home on a few occasions, allowing us a chance to get away for a couple of nights. She offered that to us, without our asking. She was a Godsend.

But her question…

"How does it feel to have it all?"

When Lena asked me that, I know that my expression must have stunned her. I think I did actually go into a momentary shock. What was otherwise a free-flowing conversation, came to an abrupt halt. I know that my eyes registered fear, I think that my heart must have literally skipped a beat, my mouth hung open without my ability to utter a single word for what seemed like forever, although it was probably only a few seconds. There were so many things rushing through my veins, so much coursing through my arteries, a million thoughts converging to what was certain to be a catastrophic explosion of…mostly things I felt would be inappropriate…on a Bible study night. I had to stop the rushing, coursing and converging. It would have to wait until another time. I was neither ready to go there myself, for fear of the ugliness, nor did I believe she was ready to see what was fighting to come to the surface.

To her question…

I simply answered, "But I don't have it all."

I smiled and thankfully, she released me from having to explain what she had just only gotten a glimpse of. Lena never asked me that again, and I wonder if she even remembers asking me that question. I especially wonder if she, now herself a wife and mother with a career, can relate… to having it all.

As mothers, I think that we all have those times of being overwhelmed in our doing, in our being, in our just trying to get by. For me, at that particular time with Lena, I was unable to articulate what I was feeling. Physically, I was just tired…working long hours with a long commute, having full weekends with the kid's activities, never-ending housework, maintaining my marriage, church on Sundays, and volunteering in various aspect at the kid's schools, etc. Emotionally, I was still unhappy, unfulfilled, and still way off track from where I had hoped to be at this point in life. In fact, I didn't think that much of what I wanted was going to be possible with the husband that I had, with three children spread apart in age as they were, or with the career field that I had chosen. Intellectually, I knew that I was blessed beyond measure and had all of the things that really mattered. I was on a tightrope, juggling all of those balls, fearing that it could all come crashing down at any moment, and that I would fall into some abyss out of which I would not be able to return.

Now, in hindsight, I believe that what I was dealing with had a lot to do, simply, with the season that I was in. Parenting is hard. I had a great career, but would be in tears trying to make it to my children before the daycare closed. My husband was working a job that often rendered him unavailable for pickups. It was a real stress on a daily basis of getting the kids on time or having to deal with the extra daycare fees and the workers that I was holding up. I felt my only other option was not to work, eliminating daycare altogether. That meant giving up the children's extra-curricular and practically anything other than the bare necessities. And, while that option is one

Powerful Secret from ....

that I deeply considered, at a minimum, on a weekly basis, my children's academic, social and developmental success always supported that they were getting what they needed, and so I stayed the course.

There were other stresses that played into that season, as well. There was my marriage. Marriage is hard. It has seasons where you must fight to stay together and fight to stay in love. All of this seemed too much at times, until I realized that the biggest weight of all that I was carrying… was not in the seasons of motherhood or marriage, but a much more personal fight, that of finding contentment in whatever season that I was in.

I had a terrible case of comparison-itis. I was spending too much time comparing that season to a future season… one that couldn't possibly be so hard. I was comparing it to the season that I had imagined it to be, many years before, which also was not so hard. I compared myself to others in my sphere that seemed to be doing so much better with like jobs, years of experience and children, as well. I was also comparing my season to others who I knew were dealing with things that were so much worse. I worked in Oncology, so although I felt this way, I had immense guilt for my feelings, because I didn't believe that I had the right or any valid reason to be struggling. What was wrong with me and how could I fix it?

⏻   The Quote That Changed It All

The cliché of seeing a glass of liquid at the halfway mark as simply being either half full or half empty would not, alone, have made the weight of my life seem less heavy. I needed more than just positive thinking that would somehow remove my physical fatigue and emotional depletion. I knew that particular saying and many others, and I also knew that I wasn't seeing my life through the right lens, but to sum it up as positive versus negative thinking… and only that…just wasn't cutting it for me. I was tired and, often overwhelmed… and simply beginning to think that I was not those things was not going to change them and so I rejected that as an answer.

There was one reading, however, on contentment, that was truly a game changer for me. I came across a quote by Priscilla Shirer that completely changed my life. "Contentment is the equilibrium between the enjoyment of life now and the anticipation of what is to come.", [1] Whereas other statements didn't do it for me, this one did! I became very excited upon reading it, and I immediately felt some of this weight lift off of me. Something had clicked, but what? Being the analytic that I am, I was determined to identify exactly what had resonated with me and why a quote could have affected me so. Well, it turns out that Priscilla's quote didn't contradict the clichés or the premise of what positive thinking can do, after all. In fact, it supported it. And presently, I do believe that seeing a glass as half full is, in fact, what we should always strive to do, and that, in the simplest of ways, doing just that actually does represent a major coping mechanism, as well as the first step to realizing a different reality. How you view or see a situation, whether in a positive or a negative light can make all of the difference.

Powerful Secret from ....

"Contentment is equilibrium between the enjoyment of life now and the anticipation of what is to come."

But what was it specifically about that quote?

Was it just identifying my lack of contentment? No, I actually had long figured out that I wasn't content. That part wasn't hard. In fact, I was in the habit of doing what I could to try and force contentment. Mostly, I became good at pretending that what I had was exactly what I had always wanted...or at least, all that I needed. And to want something else, was to be ungrateful, therefore, I squashed those feelings as best I could.

Contentment is usually defined along the lines of being in a state of contentedness, satisfied; [having] ease of mind.$_2$ Priscilla's definition was exactly what I needed because not only did it afford this common definition of contentment, "enjoyment of life now", but it married this present state with a future state with the wonderful word of anticipation..."and the anticipation of what is to come". And that, my friend, was the clincher for me! What?! You mean I could be content and look forward with anticipation to the next season as well. Apparently, I had missed this connection. I had equated contentment merely with a current state of being (as in now) with no real connection to a future state (of what I was becoming). Somehow, it had been ingrained in me or I had understood and/or just accepted along the way, that to anticipate a change or different season, somehow cheated the current season. I was feeling immense hopelessness, not because of the difficult season that I was in, but because I was grieving the death of some still unmet hopes and dreams, when there was no reason to do that, at all. I finally accepted that contentment, for me, means enjoying my current season and being present in the beautiful mess that it may be, while not forsaking what could one day be.

This realization that I could both enjoy this present state and not forsake my future state was just the "tool" I needed to persist. Before seeing that quote, I had no answer for what I was feeling, and it resulted in me thinking contentment was a this-or-that season. Contentment is sometimes a this-and-anticipation of-that season.

Contentment - Resting in Your Season, Past Experiences Maybe the Key.

⏻ First Trimester Seasons

I did not have a hard time conceiving my first child. In fact, after being married around six months, I decided to get off of birth control pills because the hormones didn't agree with me. Because I was happily married, if I got pregnant, it wouldn't be the worse time and it would be with the right person. I discussed this with Brian, my husband, and he agreed that I could take a break. We also decided to use condoms and try the rhythm method, as we didn't want to become parents anytime soon. That was our plan and because my cycle had always been so regular, I felt assured that this plan would work.

Well, as I am sure you have guessed by now, it didn't. A few months later, while at work, I started feeling queasy and too sick to drive home. Brian came to get me and I told him

Powerful Secret from ....

that I wasn't sure what was going on. The next day, I took a pregnancy test and, to my surprise, I was pregnant. We were elated, nonetheless, and were looking forward to us two becoming three. What surprised me even more, though, was that the morning sickness never subsided. It only got worse. And it was not just at a certain time of day, but an all-day long... every... single... day event. I was diagnosed with hyperemesis gravidarum, or extreme morning sickness, that in its worst-case scenario, can lead to miscarriage. I had just started a new job and had no time to take off. And it wasn't just queasiness, I truly couldn't keep food or drink down no matter what I tried to eat or sip. I didn't know anyone who had experienced such persistent morning sickness, especially to this degree. My husband was confused, as was I, and increasingly annoyed by my declining condition. My family thought I was exaggerating my symptoms. I was terrified, depressed and I was scared.

I knew that I couldn't sustain a pregnancy with continued loss of weight and practically zero nutrition. When you don't feel well, especially with something that most people don't understand or don't believe is that big a deal, you find yourself in a very lonely place. You stop expressing that you don't feel well, because who wants to hear that day after day. People stop asking because it is apparent that you are not any different, and are possibly worse than you were the last time that they saw you. It was also lonely because of the uncertainty of that season. I didn't know how this was going to end, if or when the sickness would subside, or if I could have a healthy full-term pregnancy, without hospitalization.

"If you continue to lose weight, then I have no choice but to put you in the hospital and put a feeding tube in you," were the words of my doctor. By the time she made this statement, I had already been presented to the ER for dehydration and weighed less than 100 lbs. Additionally, I was approaching my second trimester. Those words stung because I began to feel like a complete failure as a wife and as that child's mother…maybe even as a woman. How could this be happening? Weight loss and morning sickness is acceptable and not uncommon in the first trimester, but to the degree that I was experiencing this, was concerning for all. It didn't make sense.

That was a hard season for me, my husband, and my marriage. The honeymoon was definitely over. Thankfully, in the nick of time, I had enough of a decrease in the queasiness, to be able to eat and drink just a little more than I had. It was enough of a change that on my next visit to the doctor, I had not lost any more weight which was welcomed improvement. This continued throughout the rest of my second trimester until all sickness ceased. I began to gain weight and was on track with my expected weight. I ended up delivering an 8 lb-5 oz. baby girl, at full term, that was 100% healthy without the need for my hospitalization.

That was my entrance into motherhood. It was an uncertain start, but when I saw that beautiful little girl, everything that I had gone through didn't matter in the least. I would do it again, and I did… "Every pregnancy is different," is what everyone says and what I believed, as well. "Girl pregnancies are different from boy pregnancies." With

Powerful Secret from ....

subsequent pregnancies, I hoped each time that I wouldn't have that initial morning sickness. But…I did. The morning sickness was always just as bad, in fact, worse because I had a young child that needed tending to and with my last pregnancy, two children. The difference was that I had less fear because I had no reason to believe that the sickness wouldn't stop. I had the experience from the first pregnancy from which I could draw hope. Another wonderful difference is that Brian took the sickness in stride, as well. He tended to me without the fear that had previously caused him discomfort. What a difference experience makes!

I had a hard time conceiving my second child. There was a 2-year time of infertility when I thought I couldn't have another child. We were told our next step was fertility treatments. This season was hard…until we chose contentment with the child that we had and accepted that a second biological child might not be in our future. We decided that we would consider adoption if the desire to grow our family persisted and that we would simply enjoy the daughter that we had been blessed with. Shortly after this, however, I would spontaneously bleed. It was not related to my cycle and ultimately a cervical polyp was discovered and removed. Within three months of this procedure, I was pregnant.

This second season of pregnancy was hard. But I had a satisfaction, an ease of mind…a contentedness because my initial first pregnancy experience gave me reason to hope. We rode the wave of initial diagnosis, again that of hyperemesis, but that time in a different city and state, different doctor, and a 4-year-old in tow. I lost the weight, contended with some degree of depression, but anticipated its end. And end…it did. The result was a healthy daughter that weighed 7 lbs.

My third pregnancy was different. The morning sickness would be extreme for varying amounts of time, with no reason or rhyme, and then it would cease. I remember thinking this was different indeed, maybe this was a boy. I would then have days of no sickness which was perfectly ok with me, but then I had waves of queasiness that were just…weird. I ended up miscarrying that child in the first trimester. That was a hard season. We were devastated.

I became pregnant about a year later. The morning sickness came. Same diagnosis, same loss in weight, but the pregnancy progressed. With this fourth pregnancy, I went through the morning sickness with more than just an anticipation of when it would end, but with joy in the day to day continuation of it because, for me, this was a representation of my normal. I had in my arsenal three previous pregnancies from which I could draw from. I was more than content in knowing that the consistent sickness was in line with the two full-term pregnancies, so what if that meant sickness for the first full trimester. This pregnancy resulted in my having a healthy 7 lb 3 oz son.

Contentment and hope can be found in past experiences. With my last pregnancy, I found contentment in accepting that my pregnancies were different than that of others that I knew. I rested in the knowledge that the near unbearable first trimester that I'd always experienced was worth it for me. The same is true for life's journeying. Each of our paths may be different than another's, but if the end result

188

is that we ultimately reach a desirable destination, then seeking contentment, even if that means pulling from past experiences may be just what we need to persevere through a hard season.

Seasons Do Change

Babies don't stay babies forever. Toddlers don't stay toddlers forever. Marriages evolve as do the people in them. Singles get married. The married become single again. But...Seasons change. Finding the joy in the season that you are in does involve finding contentment. However, do not confuse the search for contentment with not taking steps in preparation for future seasons. If a college degree is a goal, but your current season doesn't allow full-time school, maybe it will allow an occasional on-line class. If you are in a job that you hate, then maybe a new certification will facilitate entry into a different field. If saving money is your goal, then start with banking that merit increase or a certain doable amount a week. If writing is a goal, whenever you get the urge, then start writing. Take those steps, even if small, that can add up over time and will continue to support your future desires. Just as finding contentment in your season and anticipating the next are not mutually exclusive, neither is taking a step here and there in preparation for the next.

Contentment may also be, at times, the most difficult thing to take hold of. I understand that there are some seasons that are so hard, so unexpected, so painful, and just unbelievably unwanted and even undeserved...and therefore, finding contentment is easier said than done.

However, I do believe that if you are not intentional about it, it will almost certainly elude you. And if you are intentional, then you will find more enjoyment in these moments, hours, days, weeks, months, years.

I have shared my search for it during my season of sheer exhaustion, busyness, and unending selfless times of having very small, dependent children. I have shared my search for it during times of uncertainty and sickness during my pregnancies. I have shared my search for it during a time of infertility and miscarriage. I have had other times that I had had to seek it, as well. I expect always to be intentional about seeking out contentment even as I look ahead to better or maybe just different seasons, either wanted or unwanted. I no longer experience guilt about anticipating a change, and I plan to make the best out of whatever season I am in and whatever season presents.

I tried my best to kill the hope in me of a different season because of unnecessary guilt, and that attempted murder only made things worse. Because, what I desired to kill, refused to die, and I am so glad about it. It was hopes and dreams that initially rushed, coursed and converged when I was asked about how it felt to have it all. Because having it all was feeling like too much at the time. Having it all sometimes can mean that you have more than what you can handle. So, if being guilt free about anticipating a different season can help to lighten the load, then by all means, feel free to look towards a future season. Just don't fall victim to comparison-itis. Always seek to find and thoroughly enjoy those gifts that exist in every season, because they are there.

Contentment May Be Found in the Wellsprings of Past Experiences

Each of my pregnancies had its unique share of angst. But I was able to accept what each brought with increasing contentment based on previous experiences. If you can't find hope in the future state or it is so uncertain, then look at previous experiences. Always seek the gifts or things that bring joy into your present season. If you cannot find them, seek out someone who can help you see these gifts or whose stories help you put things in perspective. The search for contentment, by any means necessary, is the power-full secret that as a mother I am compelled to share with others.

Motherhood is the most challenging, rewarding, exhausting and exhilarating journey that I believe I could ever have embarked on. Through this journey, I have felt lost and found. I have failed and prevailed. I have been overwhelmed by both the necessary and the unnecessary. I have celebrated and grieved. But with the constant search for contentment, I am assured that I will look back and know that I was present. Seasons do change…but having contentment as a constant companion doesn't have to.

1.   (Find source of the quote in Priscilla Shirer's Resolution For Women)

2.   http://www.dictionary.com/browse/contentment

Meet: Tashara Robinson

Where do you find your POWER?

I find my power each day in my identity. I have accepted the fact that I am one with The Most High God and His Eternal Spirit. I am made in His image, therefore, I can do what He does. He healed, blessed and multiplied so that's what I do! I operate/act from this position each moment so fear is minimized, if not entirely eliminated.

Chapter 12

I Choose Me!
(The Weekend from Hell)

 Day 1- Friday night, April 6, 2012

My husband was headed out to happy hour with some friends, a common occurrence during our seventeen-year marriage.

His usual process on Friday nights was to come home after work, eat the dinner that I had prepared, ask me if I needed anything and head out to *"turn a corner"* until 2 or 3 am in the morning. Through the years, I'd complain to him about why he just *had* to go out every weekend and he would respond, angrily, "My Dad used to go out every night! At least I don't go out every night and besides, you get to stay home with the kids every day while I'm out working. I need a break!" I would then feel guilty for even complaining. So, I just "sucked it up" and tolerated his weekly *commitment* to happy hour.

This Friday night, however, he arrived home earlier than usual, around 10:30 pm. He was talking loudly and in a jovial mood, typical consequence after a few hours of libations. His attention was on the cellular phone in his hand as he sat on the couch next to our nine-year-old son, who was still awake playing his video games. After about ten minutes, I noticed that my husband had fallen asleep next to our son.

SIGH.

I was feeling a bit irritated at this regularly occurring scene, but the sound of my husband's phone brought my train of thought back to the present.

DING!

I paused for a second, wondering to myself, *"Should I pick up his phone?"*

I didn't wonder too long. I leaned over my sleeping husband and gingerly eased his cellular device from his hand.

DING!

I read the message as it appeared on the screen: *"Thank you so much for dinner. I had a good time."*

The message was from a woman, a woman I did not know. Instantly, my mind took me back to a conversation my husband and I had before we got married.

When my husband and I were dating, he introduced me to all his female friends that he'd grown up with. I also remember him telling me, "If a man has female friends that his girlfriend or wife doesn't know about, those females are just women he has slept with or women he'd like to sleep with." Of course, I concluded that *this* woman is in one of those two categories.

"Wait", my mind brings me back. "Did my husband have a *date* tonight??" I ask myself. My heart is racing and I'm breathing fast and shallow.

DING!

A picture of my husband and this woman is now showing on the screen. They are smiling like they are a happy couple. I guess they asked someone to take their picture. She doesn't look anything like me- is *this* what he prefers? I am five feet six inches, she looks to be about five feet, two inches tall. I am the shade of caramel macchiato; she is a rich, mocha color. I wear shoulder-length amber colored hair extensions and she has a short "Halle Berry" hairstyle.

My husband is still asleep. So, I begin to ask myself the age-old question any woman who has been in this situation would ask herself: *Should I call this woman?* I didn't wait for an answer.

I put my middle finger on the screen to bring up the passcode screen. I enter his passcode, go to the text messages, find her text, click on it and dial her number.

My heart is beating like a racehorse.

"Hello?", she says.

"Hi, this is Kevin's wife, Tashara. It looks like you had a date with my husband tonight?"

"Husband?! He told me he wasn't married!"

"OK, thank you." I quickly hang up the phone and wake my husband.

I am pissed off now! I wake him up, "Hey!"

"Wh... What? What?", he stammers.

"Who is this?", I push his phone in his face.

"Who is who?", he looks confused.

"It sounds like you had a date with this lady!"

"What are you talking about?", he reaches for his phone but I quickly move it away from him so he can't get to it.

"I *SAID* it sounds like you had a date tonight. I called the girl and she said you told her you were NOT married!"

"What?" He rises from the couch, where our nine-year was still playing his games. Our son had that look that all parents who've argued in front of their kids hate to see: the look of fear.

"I did not have a date. I just met that girl tonight while I was up there." He is moving towards me as I am moving backwards, still trying to get his phone out of my hands.

"I told you before: if you want to date, just let me know! If you want a girlfriend, let me know so I can get a boyfriend!" He succeeds at snatching the phone out of my hand and he quickly deletes the picture of the two of them.

SHOOT! I meant to text the picture to my cell phone before I gave the phone back to him.

I look down at our son and I tell him to go to his room. He obeys, reluctantly, still with that sad, scared look on his face. I kept thinking: *"Why does he keep doing this? He really does not love me because he keeps on doing this."*

I awakened feeling heavy, sad and trapped. I don't get out the bed immediately- I lay there thinking about what my next move should be. The questions just kept coming…

I have been at home with our three kids for all this time- fifteen years to be exact. I haven't worked in so long, what am I going to do? He makes the money and gives me a weekly allowance but he takes other women out on dates with his money?? What in the world am I doing here? Why did I do this to myself? Why did I quit my job? I went to college, too!

I think back to how I ended up here…

When we first got married, we had the conversation about me staying home to raise any children that we may have. My husband grew up in a family where his mother, a high school graduate, stayed at home for a few years to raise him and his two other siblings. She went back to work in the local school cafeteria when he was five years old. His father, who had only an eighth-grade education, worked as a machinist in the local manufacturing plant. He worked each day from four in the morning until two in the afternoon. His mom went to church with him and his siblings at least twice a week while his father did whatever he wanted to do.

My husband recalled many nights when his father would come home drunk from a night of partying and would wake the entire household with his antics- from wanting to play with kids at 3 am to getting rough with his Mom. Even still, his idea of a "perfect" family was one that operated just like his family- Mommy stayed home or at least made home the priority; Daddy worked, brought home the money, ate dinner and left each night to "hang out" until three in the morning. Friday nights were different- his father may not come home until the following Monday after his shift.

I grew up with my mother, step-father and my half-brother. My mother and step-father were high school graduates and they worked as an insurance company vice-president and a purchaser for a local hospital, respectively. My mother was a young mom- she had me when she was sixteen-years-old so she had always worked. My step-father grew up with a single mother and his older sister. He was a talented high school football player but decided to enlist in the Army right after graduation. My parents took my brother and I to church weekly, worked each day, and they both came home each night.

I could tell, however, that my Mom was the "boss." The adage, "If Mommy isn't happy, ain't nobody happy" was a real phenomenon in my home. When my Mommy was upset, the entire household knew it. I remember many arguments filled with slamming doors and raised voices. I did find myself taking my step-father's side emotionally many times because my Mom appeared so much stronger than he was. I remember thinking, *"When I leave this house, I never want to make more money than my husband because whoever makes the money, makes the rules and is the boss. I don't want to be the boss of my husband."*

I officially met my husband when we were college students at the second largest state university in Texas. I remember seeing him on campus and thinking, "I remember him, we went to high school together." We didn't hang out in the same circle of friends in high school, so I really didn't *"know"* him, I saw him more frequently in college because I was a member of a sorority that mingled with his fraternity often. Every time I'd see him, he'd always ask me, "Tashara, you gotta man?" I would answer truthfully, "Yes, I gotta man."

One day, he caught me without a man: he asked his recurring question and I finally answered, "No, I don't have a man." My husband was a popular student on campus- he was a leader in a few important organizations, he was articulate and intelligent. I thought he looked like an honorable guy, I mean he was a campus leader, so that had to be a good thing, right? He also had the one thing that I believed every man should have-confidence. Our dates consisted of the normal college activities-dinners and movies. We didn't really have any deep conversations, it was as if we were a couple shortly after we began dating.

When we did make our relationship public, I remember a few people saying, "You and *KEVIN*?!? How did that happen?" I wonder now if that should have been my first warning sign.

"Tashara!", I hear my husband yell my name from downstairs.

"Yeah!", I reply.

"We are gone."

At last, an empty house. Freedom to be sad *AND* mad if I choose to be and I didn't have to worry about any questions from any of my kids about last night. I walk briskly down the stairs, like a woman on a mission. I head into our bedroom, take a shower and I get dressed and apply my makeup. I would be heading to my sons' basketball game later so I made sure my hair, my outfit and my makeup was ON POINT. I always feel better about myself when I take the time to prepare to present myself well and I needed all the motivation I could muster today. I need to make this call.

I look for my phone and I find it in my purse on the nightstand next to my side of the bed. I enter my passcode, search for *Angela Wane* in my list of contacts and hit the dial button. Angela was a tall, attractive woman with a sassy short hair-cut and a body built like a college basketball star- long legs and torso. I met her through a college girlfriend of mine about a year earlier. I remember telling my college girlfriend that I wanted to consider becoming a corporate trainer and she thought of Angela immediately. I wanted to pick her brain on how I could break into her industry. I had been sitting on this phone number for a little while now so there was no better time than today to dial her number.

I NEEDED A JOB AS SOON AS POSSIBLE.

Her phone is ringing…

"Hello?" she says.

"Angela, this is Tashara. How are you?"

"Hey Tashara! I am doing good. How are you? You are up early on a Saturday, right?"

"Girl, I am. I hope it's not too early for you?"

"Oh no, girl, this is fine. What's going on?"

"Girl, I am finally reaching out to you after a couple of months after Darla had given me your number. I wanted to get on your calendar-I need a job pretty fast and I was hoping I could pick your brain on what you think my best approach should be."

"Got it! Tomorrow, Sunday, would be a good day for us to meet. Is Sunday good for you?"

"Girl! That is perfect! You tell me what time is best for you."

"Ok well let's shoot for 2'o clock on Sunday. Sound good?"

"That is perfect. I sure appreciate you working me into your schedule so quickly. I'll see you tomorrow!"

"Alright lady, I'll see you tomorrow."

"Oh," I blurted, "Please text me your address."

"Will do!"

I hang up the phone and I feel so accomplished, even with that phone call. I had made so many idle threats over the years about getting a job but today was no idle threat.

My mind begins to bring up more questions about last night…

Did they hold hands? What did he tell her exactly? How do you just lie about not being married? Was it that easy for him to just disown me like that? He obviously wasn't wearing his wedding ring.

The boys left early again to attend the last day of the weekend basketball tournament. I head to the kitchen to brew my coffee and head back to my room to get ready.

When I hop in our SUV, I see Kevin's tablet on the passenger side floorboard.

"Should I open…" I didn't even allow myself to finished contemplating that thought and I grab the tablet and open it quickly. I click on his social media icon and I go to the messages. It looks like he had been communicating with someone already today.

I'm breathing fast and shallow… *again…*

My husband writes to a woman: "Hey girl. I've been missing you. Where are you today?"

Woman: "Hey, I'll be working in Fort Worth tomorrow."

My husband: "Let's meet for lunch."

Woman: "That's cool."

My husband: "Alright I'll call you tomorrow."

I am seeing red right now! *And this is a different woman from Friday night, too?!* I am seething right now. I toss the tablet onto the passenger front seat and hurriedly back out of our driveway.

I drive *slightly* over the speed limit to Angela's house and I am more determined than EVER to land a job out of our meeting together. When I arrive at Angela's house, her long arms are open and she greets me with a warm hug and a

202

genuine, "How are you?"

We make small talk for a few minutes-I ask her how her work travels were going, how long she had been at her current company and I ask how our mutual friend, Darla, was doing. I'm ready to talk shop now.

"So, what are you looking to do, Tashara?" Angela asks.

"Girl, right now, I'll do *anything!* My undergraduate degree is in accounting but I am open to new roles and industries. Darla told me you were a trainer and I love training so that's why I reached out to you. What do you think my process should be if I want to land a gig in this field?"

Angela described how I should develop a course and present to a few companies at no cost just to get my foot in the door, with the hopes that I would perform well enough that the company would call me back later for a paid assignment. This isn't something I was delighted to hear, considering I wanted, no, I *NEEDED* a paying job *TODAY.*

I guess my facial expressions were displaying my thoughts because Angela stopped and asked, "Are you okay?" I tried to keep this conversation on a professional level but I couldn't keep it in any longer. I paused, took a deep breath and told her, "My marriage is on rocky ground right now so being at home with my kids with no job is not where I want or need to be right now." I bowed my head as I wiped a falling tear from my eye. Angela sighed and affirmed my decision to get a job right away. We talked about how vulnerable being a stay at home was and how keeping some "mad money" was always a good idea.

"Mad money," as my grandmother described it, was a secret stash of cash that your husband knew nothing about and that only you would have access to just in case your husband made you "mad." You would now have money to do whatever or go wherever you needed. My mind takes me back…

"My Grandmother told me that I need to keep some "mad money" around just in case you make me mad. I always shared my thoughts with my husband because I thought that's what married couples do, they share their thoughts and feelings with each other. Kevin responded, "I think that's just Satan's way of dividing us and pushing you away from me." Hmmp. Satan huh??

Angela's question brings me back, "Tashara?"

"Yeah, sorry. What did you say?"

"I said, do you feel safe in your home right now?", she repeated.

"Oh yes, I do feel safe. There is no physical violence going on, just blatant disrespect I guess, that's all."

"Well, that isn't right either."

We talked for an hour more about her plan to get me up and training quickly- names, phone numbers and topics of interest that each company may be interested in receiving some training. I thanked her for her time and her willingness to open and share her network with me. I promised her that I would do an excellent job. I gave her a long hug before I made my way to my SUV.

As I got in my truck, I received a text message from my husband, "Where are you? We are on our way home", he stated.

"I'm on my way to the house," I replied. *On my way to put you out,* I thought to myself.

The home ride home, I'm envisioning how this latest exchange is going to unfold. I just assumed it was going to be another long night of arguing and I was ready-armed with cold, hard facts about his cheating, again. I arrived home about twenty minutes later but my husband and the boys still hadn't arrived home. I grab his tablet and head straight to my room, contemplating exactly how I was going to confront Kevin about the newest woman I found out about this morning. I'm feeling like I could run through a wall, I'm so mad. I'm mad but I feel foolish at the same time: *"This isn't the first time, Tashara,"* I say to myself. *"You should be mad at yourself."*

I'm startled by the sound of the garage door opening. I hear the chatter of my boys exiting their Dad's car, slamming the car doors and I hear the *"beep, beep"* of the security system alerting me that they've entered the house. I muster up a smile, exit my room and head towards my boys to hug them. I hold them a few seconds longer than usual, feeling sorry for them. I'm feeling sorry that their family isn't as strong as I had hoped it would be.

They wiggled away from me and headed upstairs to take showers and get ready for bed, as their Dad had driven through some fast food place and fed them dinner already. I look at my husband coldly and ask him, "Can I talk to you in our room?" as I turn away from him and towards our bedroom without waiting for him to respond. He sighs heavily and follows me into the room. I grab his tablet off the bed, open it to his social media app, click on the messages and as soon as it pulls up, I show it to him and ask, "So who is this?!"

I didn't wait for an answer, I screamed at the top of my lungs, *"Get out! You don't want to be here and I don't want you here!"*

"Girl, I ain't going nowhere, this is MY house!" he yelled.

"Well, you can't say here! So, I guess you were planning to go get you 'some' tomorrow, huh? Is that what the message to this girl was about?" I asked.

"Maybe! I need help," he replied.

"You sure do!" I agreed.

⏻ ONE LAST TRY

One month later, my husband registered himself for a males only counseling weekend that would take place in Washington state. After this conference, the counselors instructed the men to home and "fully disclose" every unfaithful deed that they had participated in while married. On the one hand, I wasn't looking forward to all this new information. But on the other hand, I wanted to know everything, if anything, just to prove to myself that I wasn't crazy all those years.

Just as I suspected, his detailed recollection consisted of more of the same activity that occurred during "the weekend from hell": more women, more dates and he would take these women on dates sometimes in MY car! His "extra-marital" activities spanned the duration of our marriage.

In the months to come, my husband and I enrolled in couple's counseling and individual counseling for almost a year. I read books, attended workshops, I even tried the "7 Days of Sex Challenge", where you have sex with your husband each day for seven days straight. My husband decided not to attend his happy hours or go hang with the "fellas" for about six months. I remember him telling me, "I feel like I'm in jail! Yeah, I may have messed up but I got to live! So, you are just going to have to forgive me and move on."

We would continue to go back and forth for the next two years. We would argue then make-up again. He would "mess up" and then buy me a gift or we'd go on a vacation. I'd find a strip club receipt in his pant pocket and he'd say that the receipt wasn't his but it belonged to his business partner. I hired a private investigator and then my husband found out about that. We even had our fourth child during this chaotic time. *Talk about embarrassed?* I was ashamed to be pregnant knowing that my marriage was a mess. It took me a few months to tell anyone.

⏻ RESURRECTION DAY

When our fourth child was close to a year old, I remember being alone in my bathroom, looking at myself in the mirror. I distinctly heard these words:

"Sweet baby, we are done complaining. We are done talking to any and everyone about your marriage. You are NOT a victim. You must make a choice because I cannot

bless indecision - I do not operate that way. You know what is going on now. So, what do you choose? If you choose to stay, hold your head high, knowing that you are choosing this situation and everything that comes with it. If you choose to leave, hold your high head high knowing that you are choosing that situation and everything that comes with it.

Now: What is your decision?"

NEVER in my forty-two years of living have I ever experienced anything like this before! I heard and felt these words deep in my soul. I remember envisioning myself rise from lying on a floor, looking and feeling pitiful, helpless and weak, to a standing position with straight back, head held high, feet planted securely beneath me, looking AND feeling POWERFUL.

I remember answering the question - *"Now, what is your decision?"* In my spirit. I had chosen to leave my marriage. This was indeed a supernatural, spiritual experience for me. I began to work in a new power that I had *never* experienced.

I filed for divorce in October 2014 and moved out in July 2015. I found a job and a rental house one week before I moved out. I was scared but resolute. I didn't have all of the answers when I moved out but I moved forward anyway. I hadn't received my divorce settlement when I moved out but I had my dignity.

⏻ MY NEW IDENTITY

The word resurrect means, according to Merriam-Webster, "to bring a dead person back to life; to cause something that had ended or been forgotten or lost to exist again." "Tashara" had been dead, lost *AND* forgotten for many years. As a defibrillator is used to restore the normal heart rhythm, the demise of my marriage, unfortunately, served as the electrical shock I needed to bring my perception of myself into its proper view.

 ## I BELIEVED A LIE

I learned that our actions are based on our beliefs- what I believe to be true, I make true through my words and my actions. I believed that I lacked so much in my life and that thinking totally distorted my decision making. Basing my decisions on what I was lacking was a crucial mistake.

I decided to marry my husband, in part, because I felt I lacked something. I believed that because my parents divorced, I didn't have a family and I needed to go "make a family" for myself. My parents had each moved on and I was left standing alone. I felt like I had no place, like I didn't belong anywhere. I felt like I needed stability and security. I ignored some signs that were shown to me even before I married my husband but my rationale was, "Oh, he'll grow out of this." This thinking also convinced me to have the attitude of "I am going to stay in this marriage come hell or high water!" Now, that sounds noble on the surface but this attitude coupled with an individual who is not respecting the boundaries of a marriage is not wise.

After I completed my "inner work", I concluded that I lacked NOTHING! I lacked NO GOOD THING! How did come to that conclusion? Let me show you how…

DETERMINE WHAT YOU TRULY BELIEVE ABOUT YOURSELF AND YOUR CIRCUMSTANCES

First, I had to get quiet, get alone and ask myself, "What do you believe about yourself, Tashara?" Or, an even better question I asked myself was, "Based on the behavior you are accepting from your husband, do you believe that you deserve to be treated this way? Do you believe that are not worthy of respect?"

BAM! Yes, those are hard questions to ask oneself but they were the key to my resurrection. Although I had been "raised in the church," an honest assessment of my life concluded that I had not truly BELIEVED what the Scriptures said about my life or my identity. I did feel sad and ashamed at this revelation but the Holy Spirit ushered my mind quickly beyond that point to bring to my remembrance many of the teachings related to my identity in the Scriptures.

 ## LEARN YOUR NEW NAME

One of the first teachings brought to my memory was the story of Moses. The paraphrased version of Exodus chapter 3 verses 13 and 14 goes like this: When The Most High gave Moses the task of telling Pharaoh to "let my people go", the first question Moses asked was, "When I go to the sons of Israel and I say 'The God of your fathers has sent me to you'. Now, they may say to me 'What is His name?' What shall I say to them?" The Most High answered, "Tell them '*I AM*' has sent me to you."

I discovered that the name of the Most High is "I AM," which means "The self-existent one" or " He who is." I had been calling God's name my entire life but I didn't know it. Each time I said "I AM," I was calling His name. Each time I said, "I am happy" or "I am sad" or "I am mad," I was invoking the name of God.

The second lesson brought to my remembrance was the third commandment, "Thou shalt not take the name of The Lord your God in vain."

The definition of in vain is "without success or a result." In essence, that commandment means I should not use the name of the Lord without success or result. How does one use the name of the Lord "without success"? I learned that whatever I attach to "I AM" should match the character and essence of the Most High and if it doesn't, then I would be using the name of The Most High "without success."

Let me show you how I applied this new knowledge to my own life:

I would take a sentence that I uttered, for instance, "I am sad" or "I am not enough." Then, I would ask myself, "Does this sentence line up with The Most High's true essence or character?" I would even substitute "I am" with "He who is" in my sentence and analyze it.

For instance, instead of saying "I am sad," I'd say "He who is sad." Then, I'd ask myself, "Is this statement true of The Most High?" If the answer was no, I would then know that I was using the name of The Lord in vain or without success and I would change the sentence to match His character.

⏻ LEARN YOUR NEW MODIS OPERANDI

Modis operandi means a particular way or method of doing something. I had a new way of operating now. I no longer chose to allow my mind to wander aimlessly or think about circumstances that I didn't want to occur. Nor, did I allow my mouth to just utter careless words. The process of analyzing my words showed me how I must choose my words carefully if I want success.

"Death and life are in the power of the tongue" is a popular saying based on the scripture Proverbs 18:21. I realized that I alone could bring death or life to my life and circumstances with my words. I know it sounds like fairytale talk but to show you how powerful your words are, take a minute to recall some of the careless sentences you've stated.

"If it didn't have bad luck, I would have any luck at all!"

"I just can't catch a break!"

"I am about to have a nervous breakdown!."

Now, after you said those words, did what you say come true? I'll bet you a few dollars that it did!

Conversely, review these statements:

"I am healthy, happy and whole."

"I am peaceful, calm and content."

"I am grateful that all of my needs are met."

How does your body feel after saying these words? How does your spirit feel? See the difference?

Here is the truth: whether you believe it or not, your

212

words create your life! I am ever watchful of the words I utter concerning my life and the life of those whom I love. I saw a meme on a social media site that said, "Say what you seek until you see what you've said."

So, what are you saying about yourself and your life? Choose to speak only those things that are in alignment with the character of The Most High and watch how your life and your body responds.

ACCEPT YOUR NEW TASK

I learned that The Most or the Creator is a decision maker and if I am made in His image, then that means I am a decision maker as well. Creators create-that is what we do! We create our lives through our decisions-each and every moment of our lives we are creating. I created my marriage through my decision to enable and tolerate inappropriate, disrespectful behavior for far too long. I cannot blame my ex-husband for anything-I made decisions along the way. No one made me marry him, no one made me quit my job to stay home with my kids, no one made me do anything- I chose to do these things, regardless of how "noble" they may appear.

What decision lies before you? What troubling circumstances are you facing? May I suggest that you accept the fact that you have the power to affect change in those circumstances by making a decision. I know not all of these decision will be a piece of cake but I also know from experience that *not* making a decision wastes time and gets you nowhere.

When we accept that we are decision makers, it gives us hope-hope that we do have the power to affect change in our own lives. We aren't victims, at the mercy of someone else's treatment of us. We can make life-giving choices at any moment.

 ## WE ARE RESPONSIBLE FOR OUR ACTIONS ONLY

I learned that just like I am a powerful, decision-making being, other people are as well. My ex-husband made choices during our marriage- I didn't make him do anything! I do believe I was a good wife to him but even if he says I could have done something better, the choice to take other women out on dates was HIS choice- not mine! For years, I carried the burden of his choices- I thought to myself *"Well, maybe if I looked better or if I was a better wife in some way, he wouldn't act like this. If I am better then maybe he would treat me better."* This way of thinking is a trap and I did stay married longer than I probably should have because I was thinking this way.

I can only control my thoughts, my words and my actions… no one else's.

 ## WHAT DO YOU CHOOSE?

When I accepted in my soul that I am a powerful, decision-making being and that I can control only myself, I FELT POWERFUL!

I felt so powerful that I started to ask myself, *"What do I want?"* I had never asked myself that question before. Or, I never really *BELIEVED* that I had the power to choose and create what I wanted until now. So, what do I want?

What do I want my finances to look like?

What do I want my health to be like?

What do I want my body to look like?

What kind of relationship do I want with my children? My parents? My girlfriends?

What kind of relationship do I want with my significant other?

What kind of career would I like?

What kind of house do I want?

As I matriculated through my divorce, I received so much wisdom that I had to find a way to share it with the world. I took my journal writings and transformed them into daily videos that I record and broadcast through my social media platforms. I created a website and I began to land life coaching clients who were interested in creating a plan on how to change their lives, like I did.

I use these teachings myself each day as I am now a single, divorced, working mother. I still have fearful circumstances that arise, but I filter these circumstances through this exact process: I check my beliefs, I speak life-giving words only and I choose actions that are life-giving.

This is the stuff that POWERFUL, DECISION-MAKING BEINGS do!

Acknowledgements:

I would like to thank the POWER Moms for their dedication and contributions to the success of this project. Each one of you Powerhouses helped me to bring this vison to life. I could not have done this without you. POWER Moms will be a movement that will spark the fire in so many women around the world, and you were the initiators. I can't wait to see what's next for you.

To my husband and constant supporter Christopher Walton. You continue to pray and support every dream and idea that I have. You never complain and you're always there for me. I appreciate you for understanding the mantle that's on my life, it takes a special King to step into this role as my husband and life partner you and I are a perfect fit! I thank God for you daily.

To my Power Kids, Chris, Kai-Milan and Winter, thank you for sharing your mommy with the world. I love you three, you are my heartbeat.

To my POWER Mom, Vivian Roberts. Thank you for teaching me how to be a great Mother. You are a Godly example of Proverbs 31. You sacrificed so that I could be the woman I am today. Thank you and I love you always.

To the amazing POWER Moms that I partner with, work with, and grow with. Thank you for being an inspiration.

To my family and friends, thank you for your constant love and support!

Live Fearlessly and God Bless,

Sherrie Walton

About the Authors

Sherrie Walton

Sherrie Walton travels around the world Empowering, Connecting, and Restoring the lives of women with her message "You Can...You Will...now Go Be Fearless". She is a Conference Host, Author, Life and Relationship Expert, Talk show host and Speaker. Sherrie entered the world of Entrepreneurship over 15 years ago, and after becoming the youngest black Insurance Broker in 3 years at a Fortune 500 company, she left corporate America to become a full-time entrepreneur.

Sherrie is the founder of Sherrie Walton Consulting and Publishing Group where she helps women birth their "book dreams" and creates compilation books and platforms for women speakers, business owners, and everyday women with stories of empowerment. Sherrie is the founder of Millionaire Mommy Society and creator of the Mommy & Me Dream Bigger Tour; an International multi-city (2) day experience that teaches moms and kids how to overcome their fears, pursue their dreams, and reshape their lives.

Sherrie has received Congressional Recognition for her contributions to the City of Houston. She has also received recognition from the Mayor of Houston, honoring Women Making a Difference; Houston's 40 Under 40 Next Generation of Leaders Award; and has been recognized as an Emerging Business for the Miami Superbowl. Sherrie has been seen on Fox News, featured in CEO Mom, Essence online magazine, and various media outlets.

Dr. LaTonya Woodson

La Tonya brings over 18 years of Human Resources experience to her current role as a Talent Acquisition Manager where she is responsible for on boarding, social media and diversity and inclusion. She also owns The Company Doctor, a consulting firm that offers training and professional development support and speaker services to individuals and businesses of all sizes. La Tonya has primarily worked in the private sector for Fortune 500 companies and most recently, she transitioned to higher education as an HR manager at one of the largest universities in Texas. In her previous roles, La Tonya contributed her expertise in the areas of Leadership Development, Organizational Development, Learning and Development and Employee Engagement. Her experience also includes recruiting, career development, employee relations, diversity management and executive coaching.

La Tonya uses her talents as a motivational/keynote speaker at seminars, retreats and conferences. She is actively engaged in her community, including serving on non-profit boards, participating in member-based organizations and volunteering in community/civic activities. As an elected official, she also serves as a Board Trustee for the Crowley Independent School District. She received a BS in Speech Communications from Texas Christian University, an MS in Human Resources Management and Training and Development from Amberton University and a PhD in Applied Training, Performance Improvement from the University of North Texas.

Jaquithia Stinson

Jaquithia Stinson is a God-fearing woman, devoted wife, and loving mother. She and her husband Adrian have been together for 17 years and married for 11 of those years. They share three beautiful kids Ashton (8), Alaia (10), and Adrienne (16). While being a wife and mother often takes precedent and sometimes defines her life there is much more to Mrs. Stinson. Jaquithia also has an MBA in Business Administration, a full-time job, owns a A Touch of Class fashion boutique, and runs her 10 year old daughters non-profit organization, Let's Start Giving Foundation.

Jaquithia also currently works in the City's Office of Homeless Solutions. Whether administering contracts for the City or working through the grass root approach via her non-profit, Jaquithia spends a lot of her time providing products and/or services to the homeless.

Shantania Leggins

Shantania Leggins is a professional financial empowerment coach whose passion is helping women, both married and single, reach their full potential in the area of finances. A native of New Orleans, Louisiana, she currently resides in Katy, Texas. Mrs. Leggins is married to her high school sweetheart and they have five wonderful kids.

Shantania is the founder of Wealth and Elegance an organization. She has been in the financial services industry for the past 17 years. During this time she has worked in the area of Public Accounting for firms such as Deloitte and Touche and power provider Entergy, Inc. Leggins is excited

220

that she along with her team of licensed and certified financial professionals are building a thriving organization aimed at women and families in financial services matters.

Mary Smith

Mary Smith, Mom, Mimi. Or Ms. Mary is a certified teacher in Special Education, an encourager, and motivator. Her passion is learning, as she considers herself a lifelong learner. Many of her students called her mama, so the number of "children" that she had each year multiplied tremendously. Her goal has always been to shape young minds to be successful from elementary school and beyond. After nearly twenty years as a teacher, she decided to pursue another challenge and become a mentor to other teachers.

After 13 years of marriage, she found herself a single mother with three young children. Uncertain of what to do next, she vowed to take her newfound journey day by day. She enrolled in Junior College and fell in love with education. Education would be the stepping-stone to create the life that she always wanted. It is her dream to encourage and inspire other single moms, until they are fully confident, they can make it. By bettering herself, she was able to raise three successful adult children.

Dr. Kanini Brooks

Originally from Milwaukee, Wisconsin, Dr. Kanini W. Brooks left for college after high school and has been on a journey ever since. After completing a Mathematics undergraduate degree at Spelman College in Atlanta, Georgia and a graduate degree in Mechanical Engineering at the University of Wisconsin-Madison, she found herself in Fort Worth, Texas beginning her professional career. Since then, Kanini has worked in education, training, project management, process improvement, product development, and analysis.

Kanini prides herself in helping students; she founded the Student Retention Conference at the University of Wisconsin-Madison to provide support to undergraduate students. She has also served as Co-President of the Black Graduate and Professional Students Organization. While at the University of North Texas, she founded a similar program as president of the College of Education's Doctoral Student Association at the University of North Texas. She has served on the Bond Advisory Council for Arlington ISD, participated with the Lake Como Neighborhood Alliance Council in Fort Worth. Dr. Brooks is married to Reverend Nolan Brooks of Como, Texas, and they have two teenaged children: Jalen and Kaia.

Trina Smith

Trina is an exceptional Teacher with a genuine love for people. With her servant's heart she is a stranger to none. Trina grew up attending Holy Tabernacle Church of God in Christ, Fort Worth, Texas. In 1986, when she was 9 years old, she became a born-again believer. At Holy Tabernacle Church, she served as a member of Youth Praise & Worship Team, a teacher in the Children's Church, the Assistant Nursery Director and the Youth Department Activity Head. Trina Smith has also served as the Director of Kidz ON TOP Children's Ministry at Tabernacle of Praise Church in Benbrook, Texas; under the leadership of Bishop Gary Oliver.

222

Trina Smith and her husband founded VOH Ministries Inc., in December 2011 and she is currently serving as the First Lady and Director of the Women of Greatness and the Fearless Girls Rock Organization. This year, Trina was awarded the 2017 Bridge Award for her outstanding community service impacting lives of young ladies of all ages.

Shirley Walker-King

Shirley Walker-King is a Business and Relationship Consultant, Talk Show Host, Speaker and Community Mom who possesses a wealth of knowledge, experience and expertise in human resource management, building better relationships, and empowering women to live their best life! Shirley is the CEO of SWK Management and Consulting Service, has a Bachelor's degree in Human Relations & Business, is a certified Mediator, Family Wellness Instructor, Franklin Covey Facilitator and the Cofounder of Community Mom Community Dad Inc.

Shirley has been married to Vincent King for 25 years and enjoys conducting relationship workshops with him. Shirley also works alongside her daughter, Valencia King at KKVI Radio as a Talk Show Host and Program Director. Together they conduct a workshop called M.A.D.E. Mother and Daughter Enrichment. Shirley has been seen on The Dr. Phil Show, featured on WFAA news, Resurrection Impact Ministries TV Show, Dream Big Dallas and numerous radio shows discussing family, business and personal growth. You can connect with Shirley on Social Media @swalkerking.

Shakeena Brantley, LCSW

Shakeena D. Brantley is a Licensed Clinical Social Worker. She is the founder and CEO of 3 Cord Counseling, LLC- a leading-edge counseling practice. 3 Cord Counseling LLC. is a practice that combines faith and clinical knowledge producing amazing results. Shakeena has a Masters Degree in Social Work from Florida International University, Miami, FL and a Bachelors of Science Degree in Social Psychology from Florida Atlantic University, Boca Raton, FL. She is married to a lovely and God-fearing husband and their union has been blessed with 3 beautiful children.

Inspiring, empowering, respectful, and kind, her work is dedicated to helping couples. For over a decade, she has specialized in helping Dating, Engaged/Premarital, and Married couples through their toughest times. She is an enthusiastic relationship Counselor who gains great joy in speaking strength into couples. Shakeena is a dynamic marriage counselor and speaker who also aspires to equip relationships with the tools needed.

Katrina Hudson

Katrina Hudson is a Miami, Florida native. She is an Entrepreneur, Budding Author and single mother of 3 beautiful children. Ms. Hudson is the Founder and CEO of Hudson Bayzzle Collection LLC., a fashion line dedicated to her late godmother, who lost her battle with cancer. Ms. Hudson uses her platform to motivate and encourage other women. She also strives to impact her community by finding resources to help with ongoing issues with homelessness, and at-risk youth.

Ms. Hudson has worked as a Correctional Officer and Administrative Assistant. Ms. Hudson, sharpened her organizational skills, attention to detail and the ability to work with speed and accuracy by assisting business owner Mahaqni SL. She worked diligently and faithfully behind the scenes of Mahaqni's infamous fashion shows and sold out play Hair Drama. Ms. Hudson, has worn many hats in her career as she is an amazing team player.

Anita Bowman Roussel

Anita is a lifelong learner and a personal growth and development enthusiast. She holds a BS in Medical Technology from Louisiana State University, an MBA with a Healthcare Management Focus from the University of Phoenix and has 25 years of healthcare work experience. She has been afforded opportunities to serve others in her career, church and community and now chooses to do so through her writing. Having been impacted by the sharing and transparency of others, she is determined to transparently share with others, in an effort to positively impact, as well. She believes that life is fleeting and that one should take the time to enjoy the journey rather than just focusing only on certain destinations. Her passion lies both in sharing her stories as well as encouraging others to do the same. She is a native of Northwest Louisiana and a current 20-year resident of the Dallas Fort Worth area in North Texas. She has been married to her best friend Brian for 24 years and they have three children.

Tashara Robinson

Tashara is a mother, author and speaker who hails from Dallas, Texas. She is a graduate of Skyline High School and Texas A&M University-College Station. Tashara was very active during her college days- she was a member of the inaugural Aggie Dance Team and she was a member of Alpha Kappa Alpha Sorority, Inc. Tashara believed that if she followed the "perfect life plan"-graduate college, get married, be a stay-at-home Mom-she would be happy. Life didn't work out as planned- Tashara was divorced after 19 years of marriage. The years leading up to and after her divorce were the most difficult, yet the most rewarding. Those years were filled with fear, self-doubt, peace, poise and, eventually, POWER. Her journey of self-discovery yielded a plethora of wisdom that she just could not contain. So, she began sharing with the world through her speaking engagements, website (tasharajrobinson.com), books, and her daily video podcasts entitled "Powerful Ones".